Poetic Reflections

Francis B. Monaghan jr

Poetic Reflections

A Missionary Remembers

Francis B. Mooneyhan Jr.

authorHOUSE®

AuthorHouse™
1663 Liberty Drive
Bloomington, IN 47403
www.authorhouse.com
Phone: 1-800-839-8640

Published by AuthorHouse   04/04/2012

ISBN: 978-1-4670-2722-9 (sc)

Library of Congress Control Number: 2011916076

For feedback and suggestion, please email: frankmooneyhan@bellsouth.net

CONTENTS

Acknowledgements

With abiding gratitude . . .

To my wife, Kitty, who gave me the inspiration to start putting my thoughts into poetry.

She worked tirelessly many hours typing, editing and arranging everything for publication.

To Jayne Bowers, who gave many hours helping to put things in order for publication.

To the missionaries on my mission who encouraged me through inspiration and support.

To my friends, cherished, but too numerous to mention, who have decorated and illumined my life.

To my family, whom I love and who loves me and overlooks all my mistakes

INTRODUCTION

My Poems

Beware to all who read these
Just wanted you to know
I'm a novice and do the best I can
I'm no Edger Allen Poe
They're about family, things and a mission
And how I feel inside
No thoughts of reaching perfection
or swelling up with pride
So those of you that read them
Won't feel the same as I
I hope that you don't find them
So bad they make you sigh.

My Wife-The Critic

In writing poems, I'm not too good
To do much better, I wish I could.

I have a wife that critiques them all
It sometimes makes me want to bawl.

When I think they sound just fine
She finds some fault within the line.

I can always hear her say,
"Let's change this word another way".

So if you think these poems are great
Give her credit-don't hesitate.

By Francis B. Mooneyhan Jr.
October 19, 2008

1

ACTIVITIES & SPECIAL OCCASIONS

Come to MIA
1970 Youth Camp
A Southern Youth Conference
Philmont Scout Ranch
George and Eunice
Mooneyhan Reunion
Frank and Kitty 50 Years Together
Bobby and Lisa 25th Anniversary
A Special Day
A Special Baptism
Food and Fun
Oct 8th Anniversary
Anytime For a Picnic
Road Trip Picnic
Lab Christmas Party
Another Christmas Party
Christmas Dinner
Another Meal
Group Family Home Evening
Ward Christmas Party 2009
A New Year is Here 2011

COME TO MIA

It's Wednesday evening USA
Meet all your friends at MIA
A balanced program for the youth
To play and sing and learn the truth

Christ's true church has been restored.
What it has to offer can't be ignored
The Lord, Himself, has set the way
For us to follow day by day

There's spiritual feeding, sports and fun
There's something here for every one.
Young and old can find their way.
So come on out to MIA.

Francis B. Mooneyhan Jr.
Circa 1960s

1976 YOUTH CAMP

On. June 11th at a quarter till five
We started out on a long hard drive.

Headed for the mountains of North Carolina
Not another campground could be finer.

We got, our sites to hook up
Kitty had trouble with the stick shift truck.

Our cabins were nestled way back in the trees.
We shared it all with the bugs and the bees.

All the girls were edgy — they hadn't slept much.
Stayed up the night before with girl talk and such.

Some were homesick for mommy and dad.
Some were still sleepy and some just felt bad.

No sleep the first night for hardly anyone
The lights on and off to the toilets they'd run.

Too much cookies in the bag they had delved.
And some of them scared to sleep by themselves.

The next day was better with the classes they took.
And all the camp was run by the book.

The meals weren't great but still not bad.
We had to eat it, as it was all that we had.

There was swimming and tennis and waterslides too
In fact, there was quite a lot we could do.

The fun thing for most was to visit the store.
We would eat all the goodies and go back for more.

Seminars were held all the daylong
With plenty of teaching and plenty of song.

We learned quite a lot by the group from out west
But most of the girls liked the free time the best.

We made lots of friends and had lots of fun
Joined in the activities till daylight was done.

By Francis B. Mooneyhan Jr.

A SOUTHERN YOUTH CONFERENCE

I've been told to teach the youth
And that I've tried to do
I've tried to go the extra mile
Because I've wanted to.

So it came as no surprise to me
To find my hand held high
To chaperon the youth once more
I said that I would try.

The day was hot when we all met
To catch the bus that day
The bus was late but then it came
And we got under way.

The air inside the bus went off
It didn't bother them at all
Their spirits high, they talked with
friends
And really had a ball.

We reached our destination safe
And registered everyone,
Unpacked our bags and settled down
We thought that we were done.

But not quite so, I soon found out
The day had just begun.
We gathered with all the stakes
And really had some fun.

Instructions given—skits and such
As we all anticipated.
The youth joined in though
unprepared
And each participated.

We were told there would be a dance
For all to get acquainted.
I heard a sigh and looked around
To see if a chaperon had fainted.

By midnight we had settled in
And all was snug in bed.
6 A.M. would come quite soon
And good times lay ahead.

Saturday was fun day.
We gathered in the sun.
Swimming, track and field, a dance
And everyone had fun.

Then Sunday, the day of rest
Oh what a day for me.
It started off at 9 a. m.
And what a sight to see.

All dressed up in their Sunday best
They came with shinning faces.
All the youth were ready
Each one to take their places.

The spirit of God was everywhere
In every class we met.
Not uncommon sights to see
That many eyes were wet.

All of us had fasted long.
Then came the spiritual feeding.
Everyone would meet together
For a testimony meeting.

I wish that every man could see
And every ear could hear
I wish that every heart could feel
Their testimonies dear.

These dear young teens—their
faces wet
And standing on their feet
Pouring out their hearts to God
With messages so sweet.

I'm sure the angels stood in
reverence
For the spirit of God was near
And Heavenly choirs were silenced
So all up there could hear.

One by one each teen stood up.
They were standing up for God.
Each had learned their lesson well
And holding to the iron rod.

I too had learned my lesson well.
All of my pride was gone.
I was greatly humbled by these
youth
A long way off from home.

I thought at times my heart would
burst
I felt I was on fire.
Through it all I could almost hear
The sound of a Heavenly choir.

The meeting ended all too soon
For it was time to eat
And as we broke our fast that day
We felt the spirit sweet.

7 PM was a fireside.
The day wasn't over yet.
Because before the day was done
Many an eye would be wet.

12 hours we had been in church.
I bet you think that's rough.
Not so for these kids—
They hadn't had enough.

Cottage meeting was to come.
One more meeting we had to make.
They wanted to finish testimonies
And did it as a stake.

President Black and his
counselors too,
Visitors and all the rest
Wanted this meeting to be the end
And it had to be the best.

From 10 PM till half past one
I really felt elated.
I thought it possible anytime
For our group to be translated.

Testimonies by everyone
Each standing in their places
With happy hearts and tear stained
cheeks
And smiles upon their faces.

6

To hear a teenager plead with God
To touch her father's heart
To him know and understand
That day her life would start.

To hear them plead for loving words
From parents kind and dear
To have the priesthood in their home
And have the Savior near.

To be sealed together for all time
A happy family
To live with God and Jesus Christ
For all eternity

We closed with prayer—all holding
hands
Oh what a glorious sight.
I tell you now, I'll never feel
The way I felt that night.

My heart was welded to those saints
And ever more will be.
I want be with all of them
For all eternity.

The church's future is in good hands
With youth as strong as these.
If we adults could be as strong
The Lord would be well pleased.

Unless you become as one of these
You cannot enter in.
So pure in heart and trusting God
To cleanse each one from sin.

You hear some people cut the youth
And say they aren't too much.
They say they're lazy and no good
And taking dope and such.

Some adults with puffed up pride
Think they do all the teaching
Not giving teens a 2nd thought
In all their daily preaching.

Children teach a lot each day
If we would stop and listen.
For they're not tainted by this world
If God took them home we'd miss
'um

So you adults out there take heed
If you want to know the truth
And get real close to Jesus Christ
Just listen to the youth.

By Francis B. Mooneyhan
Circa 1970

7

PHILMONT SCOUT RANCH

to the greatest crew -619-1

We shared a lot and had some fun

It wasn't easy with a heavy load

Spending hours on the road

living day by day from packs

Food and clothing in little sacks

The thrill was great from mountains high

Climbing daily to the sky

Climbing mountains – lots of looking

Finding a spot for sleep and cooking

Freeze dried food – then wash your dish

Find some time at streams to fish

Don't forget the bear bags surely

Then off to bed – 5 am comes early

We ached at every joint and pain

And yet got up and climbed again

The clear blue sky and meadows green

And other sights we'd never seen

Wild animals around us everywhere

Hanging food away from bears

New experiences where ever we go
All these things to help us grow
Hiking all day with sweat and strain
Bodies all aching and wrecked with pain

Getting lost? There's no way
Our map and compass show the way
Sometimes trails do disappear
But we always seem to find them near

Rock climbing or repelling—don't look down
A neat experience but let safety abound
Chilly nights and nice warm days
Ice cold streams along the way

Philmont Scout Ranch in the west
200 square miles—hiking at it's best
Visiting mining towns of old
Panning all the streams for gold

Burro racing—hey that's neat
Watch that they don't stomp your feet
Peach cobblers and lemon pies
All of this beneath the skies

Branding boots and cowboy songs
Asking us to sing along
Adobe bricks-you mix the straw
Dirt floor canteen—all this we saw

Black powder rifles—pack your load
Branding boots for trail or road
Indian stories—ghost tales too
They sound so real—they may be true

To David, David, Tim and Paul
Robin Andy, Matt and all
I wish the very best for you
And give my thanks to all the crew

You've all been great most every day
Lifting my spirits along the way
In all my days beneath the skies
I've never hiked with nicer guys

By Francis B. Mooneyhan Jr.
July 24, 1981

GEORGE AND EUNICE—
50 YEARS TOGETHER

In nineteen hundred and forty seven
George thought that he'd died and gone to heaven.
He found this girl from Hartsville town
The cutest thing from all around.
The best he'd seen in all his life
He knew she had to be his wife.
Many years have come and gone
And neither one has been alone
They've been together through thick 'n thin
Never borrowing—although they lend
It takes a lot to stay together
Through good and bad and stormy weather
Three things, I know that helped them win
Teri, Rita Fay and Lynn
Three lovely daughters make them proud
To push away each stormy cloud.
There's been bad and good years too
But both of them have been true blue
Strong minds each one to choose his way
To do or not to do each day.
George chose his way to camp and fish
But Eunice said, "I can't choose this".
And many a day on Santee Lake
George would fish in the Sun and bake.
The price two hundred dollars a pound
But he never let that get him down.
The very next day he'd try again
He always had another plan.
Some say he was quite good at this
But he never could teach me how to fish.
A better friend I've never had.
I feel that I could call him dad.
I love this man and always will
I'll stand by him now and until
50 more years come and then
I know that we will still be friends.

By Francis B. Mooneyhan Jr.
February 1997

Mooneyhan Reunion October 10, 1999

It's that time of year again
For making all your plans
And thinking of reunion time
With all the Mooneyhans

Goodale State Park at 1:00
Bring family and good mood.
We'll have the ice, cups, forks and spoons
And plates to hold your food
Sometimes our tastes are different
So bring your favorite drink
It might be better than the one I might think.

We want to link our family
To the genealogy tree.
We're working on a book
To see who's kin to you and me.
Bring your family group sheet
Or send by next day's mail
You're important to our tie in
So please oh please don't fail.

Please make your plans to be there.
We welcome everyone
To eat good food and chat with friends
And have some family fun

By Francis B. Mooneyhan Jr.
October 10, 1999

FRANK AND KITTY—50 YEARS TOGETHER

Fifty years is a mighty long time
To spend with one little gal
All in all it's been really great
Because she's my very best pal.

When you first get together It's all hugs and kisses
And everything's in a whirl
But as time goes on and things settle down
You're glad to have that sweet girl.

We planned things together and really had fun
A little bit of heaven
A family developed one, two, three, four,
Five six and seven.

What great fun we had vacationing and camping
Everywhere we went
Although we weren't rich, we didn't know it
And didn't regret one red cent.

Now the children are grown—scattered all over the place
And we're left almost alone
We've started enjoying our grandchildren now
As we rest in our retirement home

We're now getting older-our health is bad
But that doesn't mean a thing.
We have lots of blessings and enjoy being together
Always looking for spring.

Fifty years has been great
It's made us strong and hardy
We've amassed lots of friends
We're glad you're here-lets really have a party.

By Francis B. Mooneyhan Jr.
October 2004

13

BOBBY AND LISA'S 25TH ANNIVERSARY

From Megan, Denis, Dawn and Chad
Congratulations Mom and Dad
25 years is a mighty long time
But from all of us, it's been real fine.

We've never doubted how much you care
Because we know that you've been fair.
We've felt your sacrifice and love
And know it's like that from above.

Sometimes things were tough but came out OK
And we're much better off for it today.
Don't worry Mom and Dad—you did your part
And we want to say with all our heart

Happy Anniversary
We love you

Another voice from up above
Thanks Mom and Dad for all your love
Though I'm not present—my spirit's there
It's good to know that you still care

And in my very special way
I'm thankful for this special day.
Along with you I'll celebrate
This day with you—so make it great!

So celebrate—I shout with glee
To have you share this day with me.

By Francis B. Mooneyhan
October 2007

14

A SPECIAL DAY

February 14th is a special day
That's set aside to clear the way

The way for us to express our love
To the special ones sent from above

We've been hit by cupid's darts
To our wives and dear sweethearts

The day is set-aside for them
To cater to they're every whim

Because they're special, want them to know
How much they're loved and cared for so

It doesn't take a day each year
We hold each day with them so dear

We hold them close never to depart
Our own very special dear sweetheart.

By Francis B. Mooneyhan Jr.
February 13, 2008

A SPECIAL BABTISM

A special Baptism for Maren
A wonderful girl
To me you are the nicest and sweetest
In the whole wide world

You're eight years old
What a wonderful year
You're older and smarter
That makes you so dear

You're precious and pretty
And so very nice
Getting ready for baptism
And accepting Christ

He loves you like I do
Except so much more
He's waiting to give blessings
And many things more

So pray to Him nightly
By your bedside you kneel
Your prayers will be answered
And His love you will feel

With Christ and your PaPa,
Your dad and your mom
Two sisters and grandmas
How can you go wrong?

Though I'm not there beside you,
My spirit is there
And I send you my blessings,
My love and a prayer.

By Francis B. Mooneyhan Jr.
2008

FOOD AND FUN

They say that through a man's stomach
You'll get right to his heart.
Since I've been on my mission
That's been true right from the start.

Since the first week I've been here
To keep us in a real good mood
They've tried their best to keep us happy
I've been indulged with much great food.

A welcome party when you arrive
Farewell party when you leave
When sick, you're brought more food
To help so you don't grieve

'This is the Place Monument' party
For all the missionaries
To make it special for us
They invited dignitaries.

Behind the library a picnic
For all who work in there
Thoughtfully prepared to treat us
And served with love and care

Then there are our good friends
To welcome us aboard
I wonder how many more pounds
This old body can afford.

I'm not complaining—mind you
The days go by so fast.
Life really seems more pleasant
As we forget the past.

We work hard on our mission
Tired when day's work is done
There's nothing in the handbook
That says we can't have fun.

By Frances B. Mooneyhan Jr.
September 2008

Anniversary—October 8th

8th October
Is a very special date
That's when I made it legal
For my eternal mate.

She seventeen
And I twenty-three
I snatched her up early
While she was still free.

When you see a rare jewel
You don't wait around
For my girl
Was the pick of the town

Over the years
She's proven it true
In all of her actions
Everything she would do.

We've raised seven children
Been a good wife and mother
I never could ask
For anything other.

I've never been bored
She has personality and charm
She's wonderfully sweet
Charitable and warm.

She's a sweet spiritual person
Always thinking of Christ
Would I pick her again?
I wouldn't think twice.

8th October
Two thousand and eight
Is a very good reason
For us to celebrate.

We're still together
After all these years
We've been very happy
With very few tears.

Though we're out of town
And a long way from home
We have each other
So we don't feel alone.

Many years have passed
And we're both getting older
It's so nice to have you
To lean on my shoulder.

You're so very nice
And such a great treasure
When we're together
You bring me much pleasure.

So happy 54th anniversary
I'm glad we're alive
Looking forward to another
To make it fifty-five.

By Francis B. Mooneyhan Jr.
October 8, 2008

Anytime For Picnics

There's a time for everything
To make us feel good <u>inside</u>.
There's nothing like a picnic
To get us all <u>outside</u>.

The air is clean and fresh
Sitting underneath the trees
Feel the pressure on our faces
Coming from the breeze.

Lots of food for appetite
Surrounded by good friends.
The benefits for picnics
Seem to never end.

We leave our worries all at home
Just relax, enjoy the mood
Unwind from all our troubles
Enjoy nature and the food.

All seasons are good for picnics
Come summer or the fall
You can have fun—enjoy the sun
And just enjoy them all.

So anytime you're bothered
And have a troubled mind
Enjoy with friends a picnic
And leave your woes behind.

By Francis B. Mooneyhan
October 2008

Road Trip Picnic

We left out early—after one
To go on a picnic and have some fun.
Mike and Sheila, Gloria, Pam,
Frank and Kitty leaving Town.

Heading south towards Provo
Into the mountains we would go.
Timpanogos range, a place to find
A picnic spot to ease our mind.

Between the mountains, not too hot
In fact, was cool—our picnic spot.
It didn't bother us a bit.
In fact the food made quite a hit.

Further on through Timpanogos,
Saw many critters—but no gophers
Deer crossing with no fear
Hardly knew that we were near.

All the colors this time of year
Are very beautiful and clear
Aspen trees of green and gold
Standing out so stark and bold.

Farther south as we did go
So we could get into Provo.
Before we got there—best of all
The view of this great waterfall.

Leaving Provo, pure and simple
We saw the Tempanogos temple.
Headed home—our journey ends
It sure is nice to be with friends.

By Francis B. Mooneyhan Jr.
October 2008

LAB CHRISTMAS PARTY

It's that time of year again
With mistletoe and holly
Most of us are not too different
We too, like being jolly

We work most every day
As quietly as can be
Doing our jobs as best as we can
Without a jubilee

We drop the somber altitude
And try to change the mood
For our special Christmas party
And just enjoy the food

It's nice to get together
With good friends every year
To show love and companionship
And spread some Christmas cheer

When seasons change, and Christmas comes
There's gladness in the air
People have a change of heart
With happiness everywhere

Francis B. Mooneyhan Jr.
November 28, 2008

ANOTHER LAB CHRISTMAS PARTY

That Happy season's here again
Been working all the year
Time to slow it down a bit
And have some fun and cheer.

All our lab crew's feeling fine
With zest we feel so hardy
Eating food and singing songs
We're sure enjoying our party.

Christmas is a time of joy
To celebrate the season
Family, friends and lots of food
That gives another reason

To get together for awhile
And celebrate like this
No worries have we for a gift
Or a Christmas list.

Just enjoy association
Of each and every one
A get together all of us
To sing and have some fun.

We can't forget what brings us here
To give us such a favor
To celebrate a special day,
The birth of our dear Savior.
Christ was born to bring us joy
Hope to celebrate
All the good gifts brought to us
That we appreciate.

We love the Lord and all our
friends
And hope it stays that way
It's so nice to celebrate
Each year on Christmas day.

By Francis B. Mooneyhan Jr.
December 13, 2008

CHRISTMAS DINNER

Christmas dinner 2008
For those who didn't leave
With a snow storm headed here
We'd stay inside, more friends receive

Turkey, dressing, cranberry sauce,
Sweet potatoes, coconut pie
All the other foods we like
To please our pallets and satisfy

Jovial friends and good conversation
We all had a wonderful time
Trading stories and having fun
With no one left behind.

It's great when good friends get together
It gives us all a reason
To celebrate the birth of Christ
On this Christmas season

By Francis B. Mooneyhan Jr.
December 26, 2008

ANOTHER MEAL

On my day off
Feeling good as can feel
I was told by my wife
We had to go out for a meal.

My solitude was shattered
We had to be bold
Gather up our food
And go out in the cold.

It seemed our good missionaries
With their energy and zeal
Had joyfully planned
For yet another meal

Every time we have off
In any kind of weather
It seems they have plans
To have a meal together

Week after week
Lugging food down the street
Trying to find
A new place to eat

People would stare
From both sides of the walk
At the elders and sisters
Who like to meet, eat and talk

Though I still have my figure
And all the food is great
I don't know how much longer
Before I start to put on weight

By Francis B. Mooneyhan-January 19, 2009

Our Family Home Evening Group

Our group family home evening had its beginning
Because of the growth in our ward
A lot of new members were being baptized
Because of their love for the Lord

So many people in our large ward
It was hard to know everyone
We wanted to make new members feel welcome
We wouldn't stop until it was done.

We decided to start a Monday home evening
And invite the new members in
To get to know each new friend
Home evening was the place to begin.

So each Monday night from 6:30 'till 9
As a group we get together
Having fun and learning the gospel
In any kind of weather

Good food and fellowship
Movies, lessons and games
So much to do while being together
And now we know all of their names.

So now we have group family home evening
And each Monday the meetings change their places
We'd doing just what the prophet has asked
And having big smiles on our faces.

It feels good to learn about Jesus
And around others that feel the same
To know he loves and cares for us all
Because we trust in His Holy name.

June 2009

WARD CHRISTMAS PARTY 2009

At the ward Christmas party 2009

We gathered at the church to have a good time.

Many families were there and in a good mood

Looking forward to enjoying some really good food.

We were not disappointed we have lots of good cooks.

They're all multi-talented and also good looks.

It's time to unwind from the shopping we've done

Get together with friends and have some good fun.

There's good news too from the rumors I've heard

That Santa's coming here which is not too absurd.

The children are excited and have been all week

To sit on his lap and receive some good treats.

There's lots of good fun which I've nothing against

In the Camden ward of the Latter Day Saints.

So come on out and have a good time

At our Christmas party 2009

By Frances B. Mooneyhan Jr.
Christmas 2009

A NEW YEAR IS HERE

I'm almost 80—time to leave you draws near

A new year is here—it's 2011.
Each of our children gave me a little piece of heaven.

I've had a good life with most dreams coming true.
I have one more request from each of you.

I hate to go until I know all is well
That my family is safe—one way I can tell

Get your life in order with a temple recommend.
Then we will all together when our life here ends.

It seems there's a problem with us all in the temple
I'll ease my request some and make it more simple.

Just get your lives right with a temple recommend.
Then we'll have no regrets when life finally ends.

If all this happens, then we all can be sure
Life being with Jesus will be safe and secure

By Francis B. Mooneyhan Jr.
February 26, 2011

BIRTHDAYS
(Family & Friends)

Birthday Party
Kitty Turns 60
Happy Birthday Elder Denney
Happy Birthday Kitty
Happy Birthday Garry
Happy Birthday Dawn
Happy Birthday Aly
Happy Birthday Vic
Happy Birthday Sister Perry
Happy Birthday Frankie
Happy Birthday Ranveig
Happy Birthday Julie
One More Day
Happy Birthday Shawna
Lisa's 50th Birthday
Kitty's 74th Birthday

BIRTHDAY PARTY

I accept your invitation
To the party on the 5th
But I wonder before I leave here
Do I need to bring a gift?

I guess a cake would be in order
With a candle for each year
But with 40 candles burning
It would melt the cake, I fear.

Don't worry about your age'
You mellow like good wine.
I know, I'm way past 40
And getting better all the time

So on May 9th at 8:00
Put all the kids to bed
When us 'old folks' get together
We might wake up the dead.

I'm not much on alcohol
So I'll bring my Pepsi please
And in the wee hours of the morning
I can drive away with ease.

It's good for friends to get together
And really laugh so hardy.
I'll try to leave here and get unwound
At your 40th birthday party.

By Francis B. Mooneyhan Jr.
Circa 1990

KITTY TURNS 60

Here I sit with eyes so misty
Because my dear wife just turned sixty
Pain abides from head to rump
The dear girl just went over the hump.

When dinning out in town or yard
No one asks to see her card.
With a smile and a wink of the eye
They know that senior discounts apply.

And as she goes from day to day
It's getting harder to hide the gray.
She used to want to go and roam
But now feels more at ease at home.

Even though she's growing old
I really shouldn't be so bold.
I know someone that's older still
Who long time since went over the hill.

So I can't laugh too much, you see
All this long ago was me.
So don't feel bad—it could be worse.
You're next ride could be in a hearse.

Enjoy your friends before too late.
Live it up and celebrate.
And remember this until the end
You'll always be my dearest friend

I just want to make it clear.
I love you and happy birthday dear.

By Francis B. Mooneyhan
July 1997

HAPPY BIRTHDAY ELDER DENNEY

Happy Birthday Elder Denney
You've made it one more year.
I know that makes you happy
With just being here.

You're surrounded by good friends
All wishing you the best.
Your pleasing personality
Stands out from all the rest.

We don't know how old you are.
It's really not an issue.
And since you move around with ease,
We don't need a tissue.

So live it up and have a ball.
Enjoy the day a plenty.
All of us are wishing you
A HAPPY BIRTHDAY, Elder Denney.

By Francis B. Mooneyhan Jr.
2008

HAPPY BIRTHDAY KITTY

Happy Birthday Kitty
The love of my heart
I love you more now
Than I did from the start

You're older and wiser
More tender and kind
You're sweeter and nicer
With a generous giving mind.

You always think of others
Trying to alleviate their pains
Without a thought of yourself
Or the getting of gains.

You've grown better with age
In all that you do.
You've been a good wife
And has always been true

The age of this birthday,
I really don't know.
But that doesn't matter
Because I love you so.

I guess, Sister Mooneyhan,
As you're appropriately known
Would now be more fitting?
As your fame has now grown.

But even as a missionary
Your demeanor's the same
The same sweet person
You don't play a game.

The love for your Savior
Has always been firm.
And the love that you've shown Him
Has never made you squirm.

Your testimony is stronger
Your faith stronger still
And Christ will always love you
As I eternally will.

By Francis B. Mooneyhan—July 2008

HAPPY BIRTHDAY GARRY

Happy Birthday to Garry
I hear you're turning fifty
To get around the way you do
I think that's really nifty.

You've given lots of fun to all
To father and to son
In fact you've always been a joy
To each and every one.

You have such love for Jesus Christ
In keeping his commands,
You've given much credit to His name
And all the Mooneyhans.

By Francis B. Mooneyhan Jr.

October 19, 2008

HAPPY BIRTHDAY DAWN

Friday, October 24, 2008
Dawn's 18, now isn't that great!
You're now legal age and on your own
But if you get in trouble, you still have Lisa Dawn.

You can go to work and get your own pad
Have some freedom from mother and dad
You can go shopping and buy a new coat
If you find the right candidate, you can go out and vote.

You're young and healthy, lanky and lean
You have it all when you're 18.
The older you are—the prettier you get
It's even possible you're not finished yet.

You're poised and beautiful and wonderfully kind
So thoughtful and sweet with a generous mind
You make everyone happy with your sweet smile
Fun to be around makes everything worthwhile.

You have a pick of the boys from all over town
It's a good feeling having them hang around.
You're easygoing and really keen
What a wonderful time to be 18.

By Francis B. Mooneyhan Jr.
October 23, 2008

HAPPY BIRTHDAY ALY

Aly is the kind of friend
You'd like to keep until the end.

Always steadfast and just true blue
Wants to do the best for you

If judging beauty, don't hesitate
To name her the best in all the states.

Has a loving heart to all she's around
Great love for her family-to you will astound

From all of this, you now can see
Just how much this granddaughter means to me.

By Francis B. Mooneyhan Jr.
December 2008

HAPPY BIRTHDAY VIC

Happy birthday Vic
You're another year older.
But I can't tell
You're getting any bolder

All the girls out there
Are still sliding by
Why don't you give them
A wink of the eye

You'll regret all of time
On a distant birthday
When you're old and feeble
And your hair has turned gray

So strike while you're young
And have a good start
To make someone
Your favorite sweetheart

If you wait—you'll be sorry
They can't be found anywhere
While you're looking
From your old rocking chair

By Francis B. Mooneyhan Jr.
January 13, 2009

HAPPY BIRTHDAY SISTER PERRY

Happy Birthday Sister Perry
You've made it one more year
Though getting older makes you worry
Just being alive makes it so dear.

You're a beautiful classy lady
And your being here makes our day
Every year you're in our presence
Helps us all along our way

Don't worry about your age, Sister
You just mellow like good wine
I know, I've followed your progress
You get better all the time.

So have a very happy birthday.
May the years get better yet
And with all your friends and loved ones
May there never be regrets.

By Francis B Mooneyhan Jr.
February 13, 2009

HAPPY BIRTHDAY FRANKIE

Happy birthday dear Frankie
You're one year older
The older you get
More responsibility to shoulder

With teenagers at home
And a family to feed
It's seems every day
There's a much greater need.

But they're all lucky
To have someone like you
With all of their problems
You know just what to do.

Whatever the problem
You can handle them all
Even if there's a big
Stock market fall

So whatever the needs
That comes your way
Hopefully will fit in
With a much better day

You're number one
Of the children of mine
And over the years
You've turned out just fine.

We're proud of your actions
As you go on your way
We just want to wish you
A happy birthday

By Francis B. Mooneyhan Jr.
March 30 2009

Ranveig Neilson—The Great One

Happy birthday Ranveig
You've made it one more year.
No matter how you did it
Every day is dear.

Celebrating your birthday
And retirement too
Means you've finally made it,
Life's been good to you.

We're all so happy for you
You've brightened many lives.
We hope all this continues
And for you a great surprise.

By Francis B. Mooneyhan Jr.
April 14, 2009

HAPPY BIRTHDAY JULIE

Happy birthday Julie—I'll not ask your age
Although you mellow like good wine
That's the way my sweet wife is
She gets sweeter all the time.

So you and Hubby put the cold cuts away
And go out on the town
Have yourselves a great time now
There's no second time around.

There is nothing more from yesterday
Although you sure can try it
Age keeps on creeping up on you
There's no way you can deny it.

So Happy Birthday—live it up
Enjoy what nature gives to you
One day you'll be old like me
In spite of all you do.

By Francis B. Mooneyhan Jr.
April 1 2009

ONE MORE DAY

Birthdays are important
It means you're still alive
With all that's happening in this world
You still need to survive.

So just be thankful for one more day
To finish what's undone
Lots to accomplish before your death
Before the victory's won

Many people you need to help
Family ties to mend
We might just have a few days left
Before this journey ends.

So may each day on earth add up
Where ever we may trod
With good deeds over bad ones
When going back to God.

By Francis B. Mooneyhan Jr.
April 1, 2009

HAPPY BIRTHDAY SHAWNA

Happy Birthday to Shawna
You're a very special gal
Wonderful, thoughtful and sweet
You're my special pal.

Always thinking of others
And never of yourself
Your kindness to others
Shows your great depth

You're a wonderful neighbor
And you're kin to me too.
All of these traits
Is why I love you

All of these good points
Is not all that I saw
But they sure make you
My special daughter-in-law

Being a good cook
Doesn't hurt things one bit
For many a day
At your table I sit.

Put all things together
And it leads me to say
To a very special person
Have a wonderful birthday.

By Francis B. Mooneyhan Jr.
June 22, 2010

LISA'S 50th BIRTHDAY

An event that occurred sure is nifty
My daughter, Lisa, just turned fifty.

You couldn't tell by her youthful demeanor
The lines on her face couldn't be cleaner.

Lovely and warm and so full of fun.
She is a delight for most everyone.

Personality plus and oh so sweet
She gets along well with all that she meets.

No more could be asked for a sweet caring friend.
She stands by them all till their problems end.

Tho her pace has slowed some, she works every day
And can handle all problems that get in her way.

She still has the pep to attend an event
Recovering quickly from the last party she went.

Fifty's not old, there's still lots you can do.
I'm looking forward to doing them with you.

So Happy Birthday Lisa, even tho we're older.
I still love the feeling as you lean on my shoulder.

By Francis B Mooneyhan Jr.
July 11, 2011

KITTY'S 74th BIRTHDAY

You're getting older day by day
I think I like it best that way.

It means I've had you one more year
To hold you close and have you near.

I'm never bored when you're around.
I love to hear your every sound.

And tho you're turning 74
I couldn't ever love you more.

Your presence near me make me glad
The greatest joy I've ever had.

So Happy Birthday one more time
It makes my life with you sublime.

By Francis B. Mooneyhan Jr.
July 5, 2011

FAMILY & FRIENDS

OH MY SON

Oh my son, now you're gone
And all of us are left alone.
Though your parting brings us pain
I know that we shall meet again.

Now Father in Heaven lives with you
One that's good and kind and true.
This Father lives up in the sky
And gives me comfort when I cry.

Fear not my daughter – he's just asleep
I've called him home with me to keep.
It's my plan that he should die
So please take comfort – do not cry.

For if he didn't come to me
Your son again you'd never see.
I've tested him and he proved true.
Now there's lots of work for you to do.

Now prove yourself and you will be
With him for all Eternity.
Time is short - don't waste the day
Then suddenly you will hear me say

Come up my daughter – take my hand
And stand beside this fine young man.
Take your rightful place with me
And all your other kin you'll see.

We'll all be together and bells will ring
Then the Heavenly Choirs will sing.
My God, my family, Chad and me
Together for Eternity.

By Francis B. Mooneyhan Jr.
2003

CHAD

He came into a family
That loved him very much
To think of imperfections
They never thought of such.

Strong and handsome, winning smile
Personality great, so lean and tall
Even from a little child
He really had it all.

All that knew him loved him
He had lots and lots of friends
When things were going great
You saw that pleasant grin.

He took an interest in all things
His senses sure were keen
With ability to learn things quickly
Even in his teens.

When all the other children
Would go outside or play
He would stay inside with older folks
To hear what they would say.

He used to talk with his granddad
Just sitting there for hours
Listening to some good advice
And blessings that were ours.

Chad never knew a stranger
Could talk or join the fun
And with his friendly laughter
Could charm most anyone.

But all good things on earth must end
For there's a better place
When Jesus calls us home to him
Then we will see His face.

Now way up in the heavens
In all the great grandize
His personality he is sharing
While there in paradise.

God has work for Chad to do
Much greater than down here
That's why He called him home so soon
So He could have him near.

God loves His children as we do
He loves us very much
That's why He always beckons us
Wants us to keep in touch.

Sometimes when He misses us
He calls from up above
So He can love and comfort us
And give us all His love.

Even though we miss Chad so
He's in our heart and prayer
He's much happier where he is,
Being with God up there.

By Francis B. Mooneyhan
September 6, 2008

MY FAMILY

I've attempted to write poetry
I can hear you say, "Oh no"!
Though I quickly will admit it
I'm no Edger Allen Poe.

I admit I'm just a country hick
With words, just fool around
But when we get a little older
There's verse in every sound.

We think of all the things we missed
When trying to make a living
And try to make up for it
With all of our misgivings.

We learn a lesson child by child
As you are learning now
Somehow we make it through the years
We really don't know how.

Doing many things together
Relax when day is done
Enjoying our vacation time
And really having fun.

Learning of our Savior's love
That ties us as a tether.
Hoping we can live with Him
A family for forever.

You've been a joy each one of you
To me, you've brought much bliss
I wouldn't trade a single day
No experiences would I miss

I'm very proud of each of you
You've excelled in your own way
You're expanding in your knowledge,
Gifts and wisdom each and every day.

By Francis B. Mooneyhan Jr.
August 29, 2008

GRANDCHILDREN

Children and grandchildren,
We have many
But that's not to say we have a plenty.

With children, we've finished
Not so with the grands
We'd love lots more for the
Mooneyhans.

7 special children and 24 grands
That makes for a really fine clan.

They're pretty much even between female and male
But this isn't quite all of the tale.

Two are now gone to make the boys 11
They left us behind and went on to Heaven.

Now it's even with girls and boys
They all bring us many great joys.

That's not all—there's more on the way
That will add to our list most any day.

The young seen more often, the older on special days
As their paths branch out, they go separate ways.

We love them and spoil them and leave discipline for dad
After visiting with us, they sometimes are bad.

If we drop in for a visit and find them pretty rowdy
We leave right away, just dropped in to say howdy.

The discipline and training, they get at home
We give them love and affection when we get them alone.

They're nice as can be and especially sweet
To grandma and grandpa, a really great treat.

Since they're so special, we owe lots to them
Can't spoil them <u>too</u> much and give in to each whim.

After all, we're examples to show them the way
We hope they will follow as they learn day by day.

We're thankful for grandkids and the path that they trod
And hope to stay as a family as we all return to God.

By Francis B. Mooneyhan Jr.-October 2008

NEIGHBORS

To our dear friends on Pebble Lane
We thought we'd drop a line
To let you know that we are well
And all is going fine.

We love and miss you, everyone
And wish that we were there
Although we're far away from you
We still do really care.

You're always in our thoughts and minds
As neighbors, you're the best
And when any of us have problems
You always pass the test.

Though we are far away from you
And another path we trod
We feel that there are times in life
When we must serve our God.

There are many ways to do this,
At home or far away
We need to be prepared to meet Him
When comes the judgment day.

There's many ways of serving
Kindness being one of them
Treat your neighbors as yourself
That way you're serving Him.

So keep the home fires burning
Be kind in every way
We hope to be back with you
In April or in May.

By Francis B. Mooneyhan
August 29, 2008

A MESSAGE FROM GRANDPA

You ask why—the answers are few
The possibilities are many
Sometimes we get answers
Sometimes we don't get any.

We're left here to ponder
The ways of God
And think of the many
Roads that we've trod.

We've strayed off many times
Not the true way we've gone
And left alone with our thoughts
Feeling all-alone.

God has His purpose
In this life for everyone
Especially for the fathers
Who has left but yet one son.

A good worthy father
Who has a great need
To rear up the righteous
And bear up his seed.

Only a son can do that
Daughters will change their name
And your family's name
Will not remain the same.

Your Family's name
Means a lot to this land
And also to the people
By the help of your dad's hand.

Think of all the good things
That your dad has done.
Now he needs the help
Of his only living son.

So why be selfish
And think only of yourself
There are plenty other things in life
That could surely use your help.

You'll find that you're most happy
When you have things to do
When you're serving others
And not thinking just of you.

Your mind is like a computer
But much more refined
It can only handle problems
One thing at a time.

So fill it with the good things
On every occasion
Then and only then you'll find
A win-win situation.

By Francis B. Mooneyhan Jr.
October 2008

CAITLYN

Caitlyn, Caitlyn—lean and lank
Really loves her Grandpa Frank
Sweet, wonderful and kind
Not a worry on her mind

She is also smart in school
Learned to live the golden rule.
She is thoughtful of everyone
To be with her is really fun.

Not too noisy—quiet as a mouse
Helps with duties around the house
She's a friend and real good pal
I really love that sweet little gal.

By Francis B. Mooneyhan
November 2008

BONNIE BLUE

She's my sweet little Bonnie Blue
And I sure do love her too.
She's so sweet, quiet and kind
No sweeter girl you'd ever find.

She's also helpful to her mom
Helps with duties all day long
Good to sisters every day
Dad and Mom like it that way.

That brainy girl—she's no fool
Always excels when she's in school
Though hard the studies, don't take their toll
She's always on the honor roll.

Always a smile upon her mug
I can't wait to get a hug.
A lot of love she will be giving
When we get home on this Thanksgiving.

By Frances B. Mooneyhan Jr.
November 2009

LEXI

Lexi, Lexi
Sweet as can be
You write poetry
Just like me.

Mine's not too good
And not too clear.
I write of things
I see and hear.

You'll be better
Right from the start.
You'll write of nature
And things of the heart.

You'll get better
As you go along
Some of your poetry
May be put into song.

No matter what,
I know you'll be great!
To watch your progress.
I can hardly wait.

You have what it takes
To be a success
And you'll stand out
From all the rest.

So give it your best
You don't have to try.
You're already
Much better than I.

By Francis B. Mooneyhan Jr. November 2008
November 2008

60

Happy Thanksgiving Neighbors

Hello, you all on Pebble Lane
Just thought we'd drop a line
To say the work is going well
And we are feeling fine.

The weather's great this time of year
In the 70's every day
With winter not too far off
We hope it stays this way.

Although this note is short
You'll know we think of you.
You're in our minds most everyday
In everything we do.

It's hard to leave good neighbors
And just pick up and run.
You think of all the good things
That they have ever done.

Your deeds have been fantastic
When tragedies arise
Your love and help is always there
And that is no surprise.

You practice Christian principles
Like treating neighbor as yourself
Not thinking that some other time
You might could use *their* help.

We hope that things are well with you
And your family's trouble free.
That eases stress for all
Especially you and me.

I'll end this note for now
Just wanted to keep in touch
Because we really miss you all
And love you very much.

If you find some faults with us
We hope that we're forgiven.
Good luck to you and may God Bless
You all on this Thanksgiving.

Frank & Kitty Mooneyhan
November, 2008

Thanksgiving Day 2008—Family & Friends

Through the woods and across the county
To Lisa and Bob's we go.
We all know the way
For Thanksgiving Day
To spend with friends we know.

We can't wait to be with kin
To meet and have some food.
We're all excited
To be invited
And get in a real good mood.

There's golden brown turkey and cranberry sauce,
Corn and pumpkin pie
Au gratin potatoes
And red ripe tomatoes
Enough to make you sigh.

It's so much fun to be with family
It's been a long time in between.
It's such a delight
To see the sight
And fulfill all our dreams

We can all be together and have good fun
Without any gifts to buy
And with Thanksgiving
There's no gift giving
It's special—now you know why.

Just sit back, relax and enjoy old friends
And each other's tales
Though some are tall
We've heard them all
Remembering without fail.

So remember this fall and Thanksgiving Day
When families and friends get together.
This is a trend
We hope never ends
We hope will go on forever.

By Francis B. Mooneyhan Jr.
November 25, 2008

FAMILY THANKSGIVING

November is a month that's great
It happens in the fall
A time for family, friends and guests
A great time for us all

The weather's great, it's not too cold
Warm days and nice cool nights
A time for family camping trips
When cuddling feels just right.

A happy time for all the family
With all a joyous mood
Get together, have some fun
And just enjoy the food

Turkey, corn, and cranberry sauce
Dressing, gravy, and pumpkin pie
To eat and talk until your full
And just sit back and sigh

No worry of a gift to buy
Just come, enjoy the fun
Enjoy the family get together
And leave when the day is done

What better month to celebrate
When family's get together
A time we never will forget
Not now or even forever

So live it up, enjoy the food
Relax in every way
Remember this in 2008
As a great thanksgiving day

Francis B. Mooneyhan Jr.
November 28, 2008

Children are jewels sent from Heaven. Lucky for us, we received seven.
Each one different but each one nice
Each one worth the sacrifice.
So happy we are to share in God's love
To accept and train those sent from above.

FRANKIE

He was # 1 to start the Clan
Of Frank and Kitty Mooneyhan
Charles Franklin was his given name
To start his good looks, charm and fame
Over time and through the years
He's brought much joy and a few tears.
We're happy he came as # 1
So glad to have him as our son.

GARRY

Garry came as # 2
So glad to have him with us too.
More joy was added to the clan.
Of frank and Kitty Mooneyhan
Garry born so meek and mild
What a pleasant joyful child
So glad you came as #2
We'll always give our love to you.

OUR CHILDREN

LISA

3 was a little girl
The sweetest thing in all the world
So nice to have a change of gender
Lisa Dawn, so sweet and tender.
She really stole my heart from me.
I loved to hold her on my knee.
Beautiful and sweet, she has grown
So glad to have her as my own.

ROBIN

Robin Kent was # 4
I really couldn't ask for more.
A really sharp, inquisitive mind
Can repair all things he finds.
Would question me on things all day.
An easy task to keep at bay.
It's been so good to have him near
Deep in my heart he's been so dear.

JEFFERY

Jeffery Lavar was next in line.
Tall, intelligent and kind
More obedient over the years
Never gave us many tears
From all the others, he was
apart.
We love that boy with all our
heart
He # 5 was good as gold
In our hearts, so close we'll
hold.

JODI

Baby doll, the next one came.
Was her daddy's favorite name.
So sweet, cuddly, Warm and
nice
Never was a sacrifice.
She has brought joy to our
home.
Hated to see her go on her own.
6 was Jodi Lynn
That girl has always been my
friend.

ELIZABETH

With children, we thought we
were done.
But Father sent another one.
He said He had one up in Heaven
That's going to make us #7
She's so sweet—she'll be the last
So you'll have to hold on fast.
Mary Elizabeth will be her name
No other child will be the same.
That's proven true right from the
start.
That little girl just stole my heart.

By Francis B. Mooneyhan Jr.
December 17, 2008

MEMORIES of CHAD

Grandchildren are great
And I love them all.
They're all very nice
As I still recall.

I had a special one
Whose name was Chad
One of the dearest
I've ever had.

Lots of times
When he was free
He would come
To visit me.

Listened quietly
In his way
Wanted to hear
What I would say.

It was nice to talk for hours
Of events so long ago.
Seemed to have an interest there
And said he'd like to know.

Those visits meant a lot to me
Sitting there together.
I will always treasure them
Forever and forever.

By Francis B. Mooneyhan Jr.
December 20, 2008

MEGAN RADVANSKY

From the moment I saw her
I knew on that day
That she was so special
And it's proven that way.

A beautiful girl
With a kind heart to match
Not many people
Can come close to that.

She has always loved me
It was shown by display
Continues to prove it
Until this very day.

She fits right in
With the rest of the order
That's why I call her
My special granddaughter.

By Francis B. Mooneyhan Jr.
December 26, 2008

DANA CAROLINE MOONEYHAN

This Dana lives so far away
In my mind she'll always stay

Distance cannot separate
The feelings that is always great.

When she was small, she'd humor me
Always sit upon my knee

All grown up and now a teen
I think that girl is really keen.

So pretty, wonderful and kind
That girl is always on my mind.

Is she special? I say YES SIR
I wish all grandkids could be like her.

By Francis B. Mooneyhan Jr.
December 25, 2008

MY SISTER SARA

Sara Lou Gandy
Oldest sister I've had
Really worked hard together
To help mother and dad

Helped with the chores
Tended siblings each day
Worked well together
In most every way

She's sweet as can be
With a kind loving heart
And it grieves me for us
To be so far apart.

I love her so much
And I think she's so dandy
I really am proud of
Sara Lou Gandy

By Francis B. Mooneyhan Jr.
December 19, 2008

MY SISTER PEGGY

Peggy Gene Graham
That sister of mine
A wonderful girl
So loving and kind

Always thinking of others
And never herself
Her kindness of others
Shows her great depth

In getting a rating
She would get an "A" plus
We're honored to have her
To be one of us

We love and adore her
And think she's so fine
I really do love
That sister of mine

By Francis B. Mooneyhan Jr.
December 19, 2008

MY SISTER LINDA

In doing genealogy
And searching family history
I knew it was possible
For another brother and sister

My wife got the idea
Like a hound dog on a trail
That she would find them
And that she wouldn't fail.

With months and months of searching
A clue she finally found
It seemed there was a connection
In another town

She made the call to verify
The conversation was a twister
It seemed she was talking to
My loving long lost sister

Since that time we've met together
And really celebrated
To set the tie that really binds
For so long we had waited

Linda Johnson is her name
And what a find was she
She's so wonderful and sweet
And means so much to me

There's nothing like a family bind
To fasten as a tether
To have a warm relationship
That must go on forever.

We didn't meet our brother yet
His life was taken young
But we will meet someday, someway
Where Heavenly angels sung

By Francis B. Mooneyhan Jr.
December 19, 2008

CHAD MEMORIES—CHRISTMAS 2008

This time of year, our memories clear
Of one we call our own
His name is Chad, a real fine lad
Who has a Heavenly home.

He gave us joy—that handsome boy
All throughout his life
In rain or Sun—his life was fun
He seemed to have no strife.

He couldn't wait to celebrate
His birthday every year
Frank and Kitty—Mom and Dad
Anniversaries same time was dear.

When other kids would play outside
He would rather stay in to listen to what was said
Sitting near so he could hear
Things we spoke or things we read.

To him was fun to live and learn
Things that adults knew
Sit and listen—eyes would glisten
As PaPa told what he would do.

On Christmas day, in his own way
A special gift is given
In memory of his precious love
Sent down to us from Heaven.

We, too, can give the way we live
To others that we love
Just be kind to those left behind
Like God does up above.

By Francis B. Mooneyhan
December 5, 2008

THINKING OF A SAD CHRISTMAS

I'm thinking of a sad Christmas
One that's tugging at my heart
As the days get nearer-your faces get dearer
Because we're all so far apart

I'm thinking of a sad Christmas
One that I'm experiencing this year
While you're celebrating—and children waiting
To see if Santa coming near

I'm thinking of a sad Christmas
With every day that passes by
May my memories linger so clear
And your faces all stay nigh

I'm thinking of a sad Christmas
Without my family, I feel blue
I can see their faces when opening cases
Of gifts sent by me and you

I'm thinking of a sad Christmas
One that I'm not there to celebrate
I'm miles away pining—while you're all combining
To have hot chocolate and some cake

I'm thinking of a sad Christmas
All my thoughts will be of you
I can hear your laughter—the very thing I'm after
To lift my spirits when I'm blue

I'm thinking of a sad Christmas
One that I hope will not repeat
For next year I'm yearning—that I'll be returning
And have all my children around my feet

I'm thinking of a sad Christmas
With every day that passes by
And I'm yearning—of a good old day returning
With the Christmas spirits high

By Frank B. Mooneyhan Jr.-December 18, 2008

MISSION FRIENDS CHRISTMAS GREETINGS

This year we've taken special care
While we're on our mission
To see that you and all of yours
Will give us your permission

To give each one our love to you
And let you know we care
Because you are such special friends
We've met most anywhere.

A thought has entered in
To the message for this year
We want to show our love for you
And send to you good cheer.

Christmas is a special time
And you are special too
That's why we want to tell
How much we think of you

Of all the choicest friends we have
We hold you each so dear.
Glad we are to associate
And work with you so near.

Just like to send our Christmas wish
And love as best we can.
We hope this year brings joy to you
From Frank and Kitty Mooneyhan

By Francis B. Mooneyhan Jr. December 10, 2008

Special Valentine—Lisa Dawn

In this year 2009
Won't you be my valentine?
You're my special Lisa Dawn
I claim you for my very own

I love you like no other one
You always did outshine the Sun

So on this 14th 2009
I need my special valentine.

Love you,
Dad

February 14, 2009

MY BABY DOLL VALENTINE

In this year 2009
Won't you be my valentine
My "Baby Doll" you'll always be
Now and through eternity
You're still so very special dear
That's why I always want you near.
I love you because you are so fine.
I'll keep you for my valentine.

Love,

Dad

By Francis B. Mooneyhan
February 14, 2009

MY SPECIAL LIITLE GIRL VALENTINE

(ELIZABETH)

In this year 2009
I need you for my valentine.
The one that means so much to me
And will throughout eternity

The one that came into this world
To be my special little girl
I'll ask you just this one more time
Forever be my valentine.

By Francis B. Mooneyhan Jr.
February 14, 2009

OUR FAMILY VALENTINES

On this special date each year
We always think of those so dear.
We look around and try to find
All those we love that come to mind

My family means so much to me
And will throughout eternity
In searching for a valentine
Our family always comes to mind.

We loved you all right from the start
You've found a place with in our heart
So in this year2009
You are all my valentine.

By Francis B Mooneyhan Jr.
February 13, 2009

FOREVER SWEETHEARTS

To my darling sweet and kind
You've always been my valentine.
I've loved you from the very start
Wanted you for my dear sweetheart

No other love can fill your place
Or match the beauty of your face
So on this day 2009
You are the greatest valentine.

Francis B. Mooneyhan Jr.
February 13, 2009

FRANK'S VALENTINES

For Kitty

Roses are red and some roses are yellow
I consider myself one lucky fellow.
I've searched the world over and looked all around
And I think that I got the sweetest in town.
So when someone says, "Be My Valentine"
I'll take my sweetheart every single time.

Daughter Lisa

It's Valentine's Day and I just couldn't wait
To tell you I love you and think you're great!
You're still my "Princess" and will be for all time
And hope for today you'll be my valentine.

Daughter Elizabeth

It's Valentine's Day and you with no Beau
I think you're special and want you to know
There's someone who loves you and thinks you're neat
So beautiful and charming and wonderfully sweet.
Maybe next Valentine's Day—one more year
You'll find someone special that you will hold dear
Until then, I hope that you'll be fine
And consider being just my Valentine.

Daughter Jodi

Today is the day when love's in the air
You find someone special and tell her you care.
You're our "Baby Doll", so sweet and so kind
And just the right daughter for our valentine.

By Francis B. Mooneyhan
February 2004

ETERNAL FAMILY

Be of good cheer little children, I have not left you
But have gone to another place
Where I up there await you
Until again I see your face.

We all can't be together
Unless on earth you all will strive
To accept Christ and keep His Laws
Do this while you're alive.

For in this life we have a choice
With whom we want to live
By obeying commandments of our God
And having Christ our sins forgive.

You cannot wait 'till life is over
To change your ways for good
To be with those you love so much,
Live each day the way you should.

By Frances B. Mooneyhan Jr.
April 1-2009

GARRY'S GOALS

To get a degree in college
Takes a lot of work.
You have to be committed
Your lessons you can't shirk.

When you're young it's not so bad.
Your memory's sharp and bright
As you get much older
You must to study day and night.

When you're old and have a family
It's gets much tougher still.
Many things require attention
You need to have a real strong will.

Desire will keep a person moving
In the goals that he has set.
With a strong determination
He won't stop till they are met.

Garry wanted an education
To get it he must try.
He set his goals and kept on pushing
Knew he could do it by and by.

May 17th 2009
We were excited for this was the time
We've waited long for this celebration.
Now was the time for Garry's graduation.

The time was ripe and it sure was nifty
Garry waited long and just turned fifty.
Education-his goal, getting a little along.
He knew he could do it and he wasn't wrong.

Some said he'd be old when came the big day.
Garry said, That's OK". I'll be old anyway.
He kept plodding along 'till he reached his goal.
Mission complete and he's not really too old.
He has set an example for me and you.
Work hard and keep at it for a dream to come true.

By Francis B. Mooneyhan
May 18th, 2009

CHOICES

I know how you are grieving
And miss your loved one very much
But that won't help the situation
And not the way to keep in touch

If you really love your grandson
Like you say you do
There are things you must accomplish
The choice is up to you.

God has called for him so early
To wait for Him in paradise
If we want to join Him there
Then we must change our lives.

That's not so very hard to manage
Just cleanse our hearts from sin.
Be more kindly to the needy
And let Christ enter in.

Be in church on Sunday
And take the Sacrament
Learn the things that you must do
And from your sins repent.

If you want to be with Jesus
And live again with Jake
You cannot around sit idle
There are choices that _you_ must make.

To inherit all that Jesus has
And live in paradise
We need to work out our salvation
And really change our lives

You make the call, it's up to you
A choice that you must make
To get involved and serve the Lord
Or never again be with Jake.

Along with other blessings
You can also have your family
Wife, children, grandchildren too
For all eternity

You grieve for one-there are others
Someday they'll be gone too
And all the love you give them now
There's nothing more that you can do.

Someday we all can be together
Being with each and every one
Before that wonderful day arrives
There's a lot of work here to be done

Jesus said to warn our neighbors
That means to warn our family too
I don't mean to sound so harsh
But I love and care for you.

By Francis B. Mooneyhan Jr.
July 20, 2009

FOREVER FRIENDS

A special couple moved away
Our friends for many years
We've shared so much together
Our laughter and our tears

Curtis and Jackie Guinn are they
Have always been our friends
From our youth, to tell the truth
I hope it never ends.

Many joys we've had for years
Held us closely as a tether
As years go by more joy it brings
Hope our friendship last forever

All of us are getting older
Pains from head to rump
These problems on us started
When we went over the hump

Though nothing has abated
The problems or the friendship
Through the service to our God
We feel a real close kinship

As time goes by, I hope it lasts
In them we have a prize
Association here on earth
And into paradise

By Francis B. Mooneyhan Jr.
July 20, 2009

FRIENDS

Joe and Ruby are our friends
And always will be until the end

For years and years so close were we
I hope it lasts for eternity

They are great, we love them so
Nice to have friends like Ruby and Joe

Ann and Flo came to our town
No nicer people have I found

Kind and gentle disposition
From California, their transition

They've adapted well here in the south
And made great friends by word of mouth

Their friendship spreads all over town
It's nice to have them both around.

Larry and Willette -so close to God
No better saints to walk this sod.

No better friends will come your way
They show their charity every day.

I sure am glad they're friends of mine
I'll cherish them throughout all time.

Home evenings we have once a week
Fellowship and friendship do I seek

Eddie and Cathy fit that bill
We love them now and always will

.

Gracious hosts are they each week.
No closer friendship could I seek.

Thad and Robbie—what a pair
They never seem to have a care.

So mellowed in their disposition
You'd think that they were on a mission.

A mission to be friends of all
If anyone needs them, they're on call.

Frances and Bob, new to our crew
But we are wild about them too.

Their love and friendship to all of us
When things go wrong, they never fuss

Though they're family, that's OK
Friendship goes much better that way.

Travis and Dahma -quiet as can be
Fit in quite well as you can see

A close nit family on home evening
Night
Huddled together, oh what a sight.

We love them both and always will
Their love and friendship gives us a thrill.

Dean Weams is happier by far
When he plays for us his favorite guitar.

He entertains us from time to time
With all his songs and poems he rhymes.

No greater friend you'd want to meet
To keep your secrets and be discreet.

By Francis Mooneyhan Jr.
July 20, 2009

MY BIRTHDAY WISH

On my 80th birthday 2011
You each can contribute to a little bit of Heaven.
Your contribution to me is so very simple
Just come serve with me in the Columbia Temple.

Each of you means so much to me
You have so much to offer for eternity.
I've enjoyed your love since the day you were born
And without you forever I would be so forlorn.

My reason for living for a very long time
To teach you of Jesus and make you all mine.
I yearn for the day when I get the great prize
And have all of you with me in paradise.

The best birthday present is so very simple
On my 80th birthday serve with me in the temple.
So get started early before it's too late
Or you'll find yourself stranded outside of the gate.

All it takes is a temple recommend
So work on the problems you think you must mend.
Don't want to lose a single one—I want with me all 7.
You've made my life on earth great—make it greater still in
Heaven.

By Francis B. Mooneyhan Jr.
August 1, 2010

SALLY ELIZABETH BLISS

We have seven children.
All have given us some grands.
Our girls are married to others,
Not all are Mooneyhans.

The latest one to add to numbers
Made the family grow some more
A sweet baby girl named Sally Bliss
Made the number twenty four

From early morn 'till late at night
She made her presence known
Kicking, pushing causing pain
She was ready to be born.

On Tuesday the 12th at 9:06
She weighed 7 pounds 11
So happy to be free on earth
Had just arrived from heaven.

She gave her mom a real hard time
She wanted an early birth.
The Lord decides the time for all
Of us to come on earth.

We're happy she came to stay with us
She came from up above
To bless all of us
And shower us with love.

By Francis B. Mooneyhan Jr.
April 12, 2011

MOTHER'S DAY 2011

It's Mothers Day 2011
And what a day it is
A little girl named Sally
Came to stay with Liz

No sweeter day can come to Moms
Than have a gift like this
She was so thrilled to have a girl
She named her Sally Bliss

Sally too was thrilled to be
On earth to have a Mother
1st Mothers Day for each of them
Hopes there will be another

Oh what a day for two sweet girls
In every kind of way
So glad for both to celebrate
On their first Mother's Day.

By Francis B. Mooneyhan Jr.
June 2011

MISSIONARY WORK

Sister McNally
Elder & Sister Denney Leaving
Elder & Sister Eldridge Heading Home
Elder & Sister Elmer Leaving
Brown's Farewell
Eduardo's Farewell
Donkergoed's Farewell
Diamond's Farewell
Ranveig Leaving
Of All The Things I've Ever Done
Final Lab Farewell
Mission Farewell
Mission Departure

Missionary Meals

In the season of love
When we think of gift giving.
Our thoughts turn to Christ
For our sins to be forgiven.

We wonder what's expected
What we can do to make amends
To pile up some points
Before this year ends.

One thing comes to mind
And it's plain as can be.
Christ said if you've done it to them
You've done it to me.

We all have our family,
Our friends and our brothers
But our missionary friends
Only have each other.

Far away from home
On this joyous season
They've left all behind
For only one reason.

To come on a mission
To help teach our friends
The truth about Christ
Before our journey here ends.

We're all held accountable
For a number of things
And can tell by our actions
By the results that it brings.

The Elders aren't good cooks
As most of you know
It's usually a sandwich
And away they go.

So please share your blessings
With others in need.
I'm asking you kindly
For the missionaries to feed.

I know that you're busy
With not much time to cook.
There are other ways of serving
With a food coupon book.

Look deep in your heart
This holiday season
And try to come up
With a really good reason

To be kind to the Elders
And show them you care.
Your blessings will double
If a meal you will share.
And
You will hear this grateful sound
As they pull out of sight
"Man! What a Great Meal"
"I can't eat another bite!"

By Francis B. Mooneyhan Jr.
1977

Elder and Sister Monson—
Complete SC Mission 1998

In fourteen hundred and ninety two
Columbus sailed the Ocean blue.
In nineteen hundred and fifty two
David and Jedda found love that's true.

Forty six years is a mighty long time
But true love helps to pass the time.
They had four girls and three boys too.
Around the house there was plenty to do.

With a large house it's hard to survive.
Hard work & determination kept them alive.
He worked out while she stayed home
But that doesn't mean that she was alone

With plenty of children she had lots to do
With cleaning & canning & cooking up stew
They all had chores with David joining in.
He didn't mind at all as he showed his big grin.

David's always happy and his big grin shows it.
He's a very lucky person and he really knows it.
With church callings they know what it's about
She in Relief Society and him in the Scouts.

As the children got older and all left home
Jedda found that she was feeling alone.
So off with the apron and off to a job
Out in the world fighting the mob.

Many years later they decided to retire
Out of the work force and out of the mire.
Retired from their work and all settled down
The Bishop called them to get out of town.

You'll go on a mission to some foreign land
The prophet will send you as far as he can
The call came in, it was foreign, you bet
South Carolina, as far as you can get

They knew so little about their new call.
They only knew it started with "Hi y'all"
To Camden they came, oh what a sight
They stayed with the Mooneyhans
Their first night.

It didn't take long for them to start teaching
The gospel to all and even some preaching.
The ward embraced them, inviting them in.
It wasn't long before we all became friends.

Full of personality and charm.
Both spiritual giants, so friendly and warm.
It's been 18 months; it's now time to leave.
To see them go, really makes us grieve.

What a special blessing to have them here.
Though gone, they'll spiritually be near.
The gospel of Christ is to love one another
And keeps us close as sister and brother.

So David and Jedda, you're never alone.
You can always make S. C. your home.

By Francis B. Mooneyhan
1998

A CALL TO SERVE

A call to serve came through our Bishop
For us to serve a mission.
I sat in awe with what was said
I scarce could hardly listen.

To leave my home and family
It really didn't seem fair.
We could stay right here and serve
That way we'd do our share.

The Lord doesn't do everything our way,
For us He knows what's best.
He wants to know if we'll obey.
He puts us to the test.

Abraham and Isaac didn't like their test
It really wasn't nice.
Obey they did and made the trip
To make the sacrifice.

The Savior made the sacrifice
Without even a whim,
So that all of us forever more
Could come and live with Him.

So who are we to drag our feet?
And not accept the call?
We know this year will be our best
And benefit us all.

Blessings come to all who serve.
We're better off this way,
Serving and obeying Him,
We'll live with Him someday.

Thanks to all of you who came
To celebrate our leaving.
Your love and friendship means a lot
And eases up our grieving.

So party up, enjoy the food, the
Friendship and the occasion.
One year from now we'll all be back
Another party we'll be raising.

By Francis B. Mooneyhan Jr.
April 2008

CALLED TO SERVE—CONTINUED

A Call to serve came to our bishop
For us to serve a mission.
I sat in awe with what was said,
I scarce could hardly listen.

How could this be?
My health is bad
Have trouble with my heart,
Can't see, can't hear, diabetes too
And that is just a start.

But loving God, I then said yes
I'd certainly try to go.
In all my years since baptism,
I'd never told Him no.

Staying home with family
Would really be so nice.
But when the Lord calls on us,
Then we must sacrifice.

So off we went
To our assignment out West.
Vowing each moment
That we'd do our best.

But when we arrived there
To my great surprise
I saw unhealthy missionaries
I couldn't believe my eyes

Wheelchairs and crutches
And all kinds of aid,
Getting assistance
From everything made.

Not asking for help,
Just serving the Lord.
Going out everyday
Obeying the word.

I felt so ashamed
With the problems I had.
When I saw their condition,
I felt really bad.

So with the blind and the cripple,
The deaf and the lame,
I'll just do my duty
And try not to complain.

There's nothing for us here
And nothing to compare
With the blessings we'll get
When we live with Christ up there.

So what are _you_ waiting for?
There's plenty to do.
The work in God's kingdom
Is depending on you.

You don't have to be perfect,
Just willing to start
With a love for your Father
And a kind willing heart.

By Francis B. Mooneyhan Jr.
May 2008

A Missionary's Surprise Calling

When you're called to serve a mission
You look forward to the call.
You feel that you're conditioned
To go out and teach them all.

But when your call comes in
You think that it's a pity
It's in the Family History library
Way out in Salt Lake City.

What kind of service could I give?
In a library of all places
Where many people come and go
With smiles upon their faces.

Why do they leave from all these books?
Supporting a big grin?
Because their search has led them
With a connection to their kin.

People come from world wide over
For reasons they don't know
They feel Elijah pushing
So searching they must go.

When the spirit touches them
They're pricked within their heart
They know not why they're searching books
But know that they must start.

Back home they wouldn't give a thought
With elders knocking on their door
Now with this new spirit in their hearts
They are eager to learn more.

Somehow the Spirit softens them
While searching for their kin.
They know not why, but they must try
To let them enter in.

With softened hearts, they then will listen
When missionaries come around.
And though they try, they know not why
They cannot turn them down.

After hearing, they accept it
Then another soul they'll save.
Not only them, but others like them
Even those within the grave.

Don't ever wonder about your calling
Although you may get strange looks.
You never know what's waiting for them
When they're searching through those books

More converts from genealogy
Than most any other way
Just be glad you got this calling
Now have a happy day.

By Francis B. Mooneyhan
October 2008

A CHANCE TO SERVE

I didn't come on my mission
For gaiety and fun
But just fulfill assignments
And get my duties done.

I have just enough strength from Him
To do my job each day
He lifts and guides and comforts me
And helps me on my way.

I'm glad to have the chance to serve
In a small way do my part
The love I have for Jesus Christ
Radiates within my heart.

By Francis B. Mooneyhan Jr.
2008

WHAT IS A MISSIONARY

Children are taught from the time of their youth
That they should go on a mission.
So they learn and save for that great day
Until they get their commission.

So where will they go, they really don't know
Maybe to Timbuktu
Or close to home in the United States
A place like Kalamazoo.

Exotic places are all in their minds
As they're eagerly awaiting their call
When the letter comes in it's opened with a grin
And then their faces fall.

It's the Genealogy Library in Salt Lake City
Is that the call for me?
How could this be called missionary work?
How oh how can it be?

We need to remember, we can't all be a prophet
Or other things we might desire
But serve we must to be with the just
To sing in the Heavenly Choir.

The feet cannot say, "I'm more important
Because I move you to and fro.
Without the legs to move you about
You would never anyplace go.

There are many parts to the gospel plan
Equally important to God.
He expects each of us to do our share
In whatever path is trod.

We need remember – there are others that are gone
That have left us long before.
They must also have a choice at salvation
They plead for it more and more.

Family members we miss deserve a chance too.
They're awaiting their ties to each other –
Needing your work for them to do
To connect them to Father and Mother.

So, without the books and research that is done
We may never complete our task.
So what is a missionary? It's the saving of souls
Other than that - you don't even need ask.

By Frank Mooneyhan - August 2008

MY MISSIONARY DUTY

My duty as a missionary
To warn my family and my friends
Teach them all of Jesus Christ
Before our journey ends.

So I must use time wisely now
Before I meet my maker
To see that all my loved ones
Of Christ's offerings, full partakers

There's work a plenty here at home
No need to travel far.
God always has a job for us
No matter where you are.

By Francis B. Mooneyhan Jr.
July 7-2009

IT DOESN'T MATTER WHERE YOU SERVE

It doesn't matter where you serve
Jesus accepts it all.
As long as you're working in His kingdom
You're working on your call.

In His kingdom we're all important
In everything we do
We all can't proselyte and teach the gospel
But there's work for me and you

Some come out to Salt Lake City
To find a way to serve
They love the Lord with all their heart
And have a lot of nerve

Using any means available
To try to make each day
Having fun and helping others
As they go on their way

But serve they must to do their share
In any way they can
To further work here in God's kingdom
In helping out their fellow man

By Francis B. Mooneyhan Jr.
Febuary 8, 2009

HEAVENLY FATER'S WORKSHOP—OUR CONSERVATION LAB

I had a great desire to serve the Lord
To go on a mission to teach His Word
So where did I go – oh what a pity
I was sent to Salt Lake City

Everyone knows they're all LDS
Out there I could _never_ have success
I was sent to the Family History Library
Closed up in a building – not too airy

What could I do for the Lord in there?
And I doubt that anyone else would care.

So I took it to the Lord
Said I'd try to find a way
To be useful in His service
And make _use of every_ day

The conservation and preservation lab
With lots and lots of books
Torn, tattered and misused badly
Much worse than first it looks.

Could there be a message here
To view in a different light?
Some way of serving, learning too
And make all things a right.

Remove bad books from off the shelf
Like separating wheat from tares
Replace with new like new converts
Showing someone really cares.

Old and used books need repairing
Is like repentances that makes us new
It seems there are parables everywhere
In everything we do.

Often the books we pull from shelves
Books both large and small
Wisdom or lacking, powerful or weak
God, _no respecter of one_
But loves and respects us all.

Serials – linking families together
Channel binding – to make strong
Maps - preserved to give direction
Encapsulating is like sealings in temples
Keeps us from going wrong.

Labeling reminds us of new names
Bar codes, of the judgment bar of Christ
Put new books back on the shelf
Gives another chance at life.

Without the _books_, the search is futile
We'd never find our kin.
We couldn't reach the higher plain
Exaltation we can't win.

So be real proud of what you do
It means a lot to God
We do our share like the great pioneers
With all the trails they trod.

Written by Frances B Mooneyhan
August 2008

OUR CONVERSATION LAB

Our Conservation Lab 2008
All that work here are really great!

Half are missionaries - half full time
That makes our lab staff really fine.

New ones coming, tutored well
Love and relationship, really swell.

Scott's in charge of all the Beat
And hey, is that guy really neat!

The place us humming day to day
And he hopes it always stays that way.

In charge of missionaries, Elder Denney
And he has work to do – A plenty.

Eduardo's busy fixings things
And correcting troubles which we bring.

Ranveig decides from all the books
Which need repairing to keep good looks.

The Rikers and the Browns are wonderful pairs
They easily fit most anywhere.

Mark, Sylvia, Diamonds, part time each week
To help in production and our up-keep.

Channel binding is needed – double fanning is grand
You'll find all this from the Mooneyhans.

The Olson's are great, multitalented are they
Nothings too much that comes their way.

Marsha and Julie is an important part
In the things that they do, and close to our heart.

Sister Denney's job will help and enable
You to find on the shelves where she has put labels.

Donkersgoad doesn't come everyday to the lab
He's an excellent craftsman, with a great gift for gab.

Locator labels which they use for a tally
Is put on the books by Sister McNally.

All in all, we're a really great crew
We've become perfected in all that we do.

We work together to accomplish our goal
Each one does their job without being told.

We know it's God's work, no matter the task
Just working each day, we don't have to be asked.

By Francis B. Mooneyhan Jr.

WHAT THEY KNOW

There's a lot of old people, as you well know.
I met a lot on my mission out west.
Well up in age and still trying
To do their very best

You would think as they age they would want to retire
And sit on the porch in a swing
But that's not the case they want to serve Christ
More than any other thing

When they're young and have children there's plenty to do
Have a job and get education
Provide for their needs-teach them the gospel
Have fun and recreation

Take them to church and learn to be wise
In decisions that's made each day
They slowly gain knowledge-learn what's important
To carry them on their way.

The older they get—they know time's running out
Somewhere this old body will lie
They're not sure, but not taking the chance
Where they'll rest bye and bye

They know that God has promised
To be with Him above
To be forgiven of all our sins
And give him all our love.

They know this is true and try with all their might
To do everything they can,
Repent of their sins, build good relations
And loving our fellow man

Instead of resting at home—they're out on a mission
Trying to do the Lord's work
Blind, crippled and pained—they do everything
Never a day from duty do they shirk.

There are never good results when you're working the day
Trying to win the prize
The greatest joy we'll ever have
Will be in paradise.

By Francis B. Mooneyhan Jr.
January 7, 2009

THE MISSIONARY BRANCH

I joined the church over 50 years ago
And attended wards worldwide
I wasn't quite prepared to see
The things where I now reside

Usually when we go to church
In cities round about
The makeup is of younger groups
With people in and out

It's not as quiet for Sacrament
As you would hope it'd be
People still learning doctrinal rules
On which they can agree

Not so in our missionary branch
Most things 100 percent
You can hear a pin drop
When partaking the Sacrament

Attendance at church 100 percent
The same for home teaching too
In fact that's the way it is
In everything we do

All in the branch are tithe payers
They learned this long ago
And since we all are missionaries
We hope our spirits grow.

I guess it's as it should be
We've had time to learn of God
And yet we're still not perfect
In church we sometimes nod.

What a glorious place to learn
And prepare for things on high
Where everything's near perfect
We still must toil and try.

If there's such a place as Zion
Out here there's just a chance
You might just find it when we serve
In this Missionary Branch

By Francis B. Mooneyhan Jr.—November 23, 2008

A Southern Missionary's Dilemma

Winter is coming
And I dread the thought
To prepare for this weather
Not enough clothing have I brought.

The winter is different
Back home in the south
Some kinds of clothing
You can easily do without.

But not in the west
Where the cold wind blows
And close up the streets
With three feet of snow.

A nice pair of grippers
Would really be nice
To hold you up steady
So you don't slip on the ice.

A good pair of warm gloves
For your hands and your fingers
To give good protection
When the cold weather lingers.

A good warm coat
And muffs for the ears
A special rain jacket
When the storm cloud appears.

So I hurry and hurry
'Till I'm out of breath
To prepare for these winters
To keep from freezing to death.

By Francis B. Mooneyhan Jr.
Fall 2008

NO MISSION IMPOSSIBLE

Long before my mission call
Had trouble with my heart
After getting up each day
I could hardly get my start.

In sitting in my room all day
Feeling very frail
It was hard for me to get outside
Even to pick up the mail

The call came from our Bishop
For us to serve a mission
I thought that odd – how can that be
A man in my condition

Away we went with my bad health
And man, was I a pity
We ended up in the genealogy library
Way out in Salt Lake City.

When you're having difficulties
And have a real hard task
Heavenly Father is waiting
All you need to do is ask.

Asked I did and lots more too
I begged for strength to serve
I knew I asked a lot of Him
It took a lot of nerve.

He listened lovingly as usual
And granted my request.
As long as I would put forth effort
And try to do my best.

Things aren't easy – they never are
But He helps us on the way
I get to work each morning
And walked it all the way.

Eight hours a day I toiled away
Employed to work for God
Trying to do the best I could
To get his gracious nod.

I made it, although I don't know how
Had troubles along the way
But not my heart – it kept on ticking
Every single day.

So never say you can't or won't
In God's work you're needed.
It may be other things than health
That's way down in you – deep seeded

Never under estimate your Father
He loves you very much.
He wants to give you blessings
But you must keep in touch.

He only asks that you will try
Repent and do your share
Work hard and live to be with Him
To show you really care.

Everything will have its price
What will you give or pay
To live with God and Jesus Christ
When comes the judgment day.

By Francis B. Mooneyhan Jr.
November, 2008

JOINING FORCES

With a new year beginning
And the old one ringing out,
A lot of new changes
Are coming about.

Two labs are now merging
To give inspiration;
The Conservation Lab
And Photo Duplication.

We will work well together,
New techniques we'll be bringing.
Especially in our devotionals
They'll add much to our singing.

Changing makes better conditions
Than how we're structured now.
The two work best together—
Better search modes to allow.

We're so happy
To be merging the crews.
All I can say is,
This really is great news.

By Francis B. Mooneyhan Jr.
January 2009

THE HARDER YOU WORK

In the family history library
Missionaries who come to work
Never in their wildest dreams
Their duties they would shirk.

Many years they've been retired
From jobs they left back home
To come out here as missionaries
And leave their families all alone.

To serve the Lord with all their heart
And work hard every day
Never time for interferences
They like it best that way.

They're working hard 8 hours a day
As busy as can be
I don't see how they keep the pace
It really puzzles me.

Have to tell them when it's time
To go home or to eat
All they have's one thing in mind
For their task to be complete.

They know just who they're working for
For years they have been learning
They harder you work for Jesus Christ
The better are your earnings.

By Francis B. Mooneyhan Jr.
February 21 2009

GENEALOGY WORK

Dear Father

Help me to have the Spirit of Elijah
In searching out my kin.
Help me understand the reason for doing it
And give me the feelings deep within.

Help me know the importance for searching
Graveyards, records and books
Talking with family or visiting court houses
To look in all of the nooks.

I love them all so dearly
They mean so much to me
Help me to prove it in the work that I do
To seal them to me eternally.

To give them a chance to learn of the gospel
To choose Christ as their own
To seal their fate and that of their family
Into our Heavenly Home.

I don't want to be slothful, I know it's important
There's plenty for me to do
Just need some help and the Spirit of Elijah
To help in this task to get through.

By Frances B. Mooneyhan Jr.
October 2008

THE FAMILY HISTORY LIBRARY

The Family History Library
It is so quiet in there.
In fact, if you wanted to
You could have yourself a prayer.

Very large rooms on every floor
With lots and lots of shelves.
Books are stacked so neatly
You can pick them out yourselves.

With all those books in there
Most are never read
But some are used and studied hard
To seek out ones that's dead.

People sitting everywhere
To check their family tree
So they can tie their families
As _one,_ eternally.

For that is what's important
God wants us all back home.
Everyone needs the gospel
So we're not left alone.

The genealogy library
It's just the place for you
It may be the most important thing
That you will ever do.

By Francis B. Mooneyhan Jr.
20 July 2008

ELDER AND SISTER ELDRIDGE

Elder Eldridge and wife have served many missions for Christ.
In fact have served in the Conservation Lab twice
They're no strangers in the work of the Lord
They sure do love preaching the word.

Though he has health problems like some of the rest
He comes in early to give of his best.
They come in early before anyone else
So they can get started and give of themselves.

Elder Eldridge is joyful and full of good cheer.
We're all so happy to have him so near.
A serious health problem to take him away
We hope he'll return quickly someday.

We know the Lord loves him and will give His permission
For he and his wife to finish their mission.
We don't need to worry, for he'll be alright
And when he returns, what a glorious sight.

By Francis B. Mooneyhan Jr.
December 3, 2008

ELDER AND SISTER ELMER

Elder and Sister Elmer
Recently came into the Lab
They're two of the finest
That we've ever had.

Brother Elmer does book repair
And quiet as can be.
But his production is great
As you will soon see.

Sister Elmer prepares books
Soon to be labeled.
So none of them ever
Have to be tabled.

Modification cataloging
Is part of her day.
She stays so busy
And likes it that way.

So between the two
We get a lot done.
Having them around
Sure makes our work fun.

By Francis B Mooneyhan Jr.
2009

RANDY HALL

We have a new member
To join our crew
He's a big help
In all that we do.

The name of this young man
Is Randy Hall.
He's really anxious
To help us all.

He's the youngest
To work in the lab I'm told
Quite a change
From the rest of the old.

He tears apart wraps
Helps take out the books
Sends BYU films
Assists in filling the nooks.

He likes running errands
Ties barcodes on books
He's all over the place
With his youth and good looks.

By Francis B. Mooneyhan Jr.
2009

WELCOME ELDER FLINDERS

As duty ends and some must leave
There's others to take their place.
Elder Flinders came into the lab
To replace another face.

He came from California
A carpenter by trade
Good at many other things
By articles he has made.

Has served four missions
And here to serve one more
Hoping by his actions
To open Heaven's door.

We're certainly glad to have him
His talents we can use.
In service to the kingdom
We never can refuse.

So welcome to our family.
We all work here as one.
We work hard each and every day
And also have some fun.

By Francis B. Mooneyhan Jr.
2009

ELDER TODD

When Elder Todd retired
Some thought he may go fishing
Instead—Elder and Sister Todd
Are serving a Family History Mission.

Sister Todd
Is a genealogist
And found herself
On the US / Canada list

Elder Todd
Is new in training
Hoping that the patience
Of Ranveig isn't straining

Being in "Family Book Repair"
And in the "Cons Lab" crew
He always will be needed there
Restoring the books like new.

By Francis B. Mooneyhan Jr.
2009

ELDER MARTINEZ WELCOME

We have another missionary
To join with all the rest.
A healthy youthful elder
With energy and zest.

He has an eager mind
And learning really fast
He fits in really well
I'm sure that he will last.

His name is Elder Martinez
He hails from Salt Lake City
Not too loud and boisterous
And yet can be quite gritty.

We hope his stay with us is long
More help we need to stay
God's kingdom here is moving fast
It's growing every day.

So welcome Elder, we're glad you're here
Glad to have you on our team
Of all the choicest ones that come
We always get the cream.

By Francis B. Mooneyhan Jr.
2009

ELDER AND SISTER BUTTARS

Elder and Sister Buttars
Recently came into our crew.
Both are multi-talented
In things that they can do.

They are filling slots
Of others moving out,
Leaving or other assignments
To do this there's no doubt.

Both are quite an asset
To our lab they bring such charm
With a pleasing personality
So pleasantly and warm.

Elder Buttars is the quiet one
Doesn't have too much to say
Except when it's important
Then it really makes the day.

Sister Buttars does more talking
She's jolly as can be
Helps the day to go by faster
With a spirit clean and free.

We welcome them with all our hearts.
They both fit in quite well.
An excellent job they do for us.
We hope they long will dwell.

By Francis B. Mooneyhan Jr.
February 17, 2009

TERI

Teri helps in the lab
And is very able
Repairs on computers
And putting on labels

Copy preservation books
As in the lab they all enter
Sends all charts and maps
To the document center

Learning new processes
Most every day
Helping to keep
The confusion at bay

Her sweetness and devotion
Is so very dear
We're all so glad
To have her work here.

By Frances B. Mooneyhan Jr.
2009

SISTER MOONEYHAN—LEAVING

Sister Mooneyhan is leaving
To work on the floor.
She won't be with us
To work here anymore.

And though we will miss her
We wish her God speed
She's learning to help others
With their genealogy needs.

We'll miss your sweet spirit
You've brought to the lab
It's one of the finest
We've ever had.

Your charm and your laughter
We'll miss very much
And hope that real often
You'll keep in touch.

So adios and goodbye
We wish you the best
We know you'll be outstanding
Among all the rest.

By Francis B. Mooneyhan Jr.
September 2008

SISTER McNALLY

Sister McNally you sure will be missed
You've been important to our team.
Every time there's been something needed
You've always been there it seems.

It's hard to compare the worth of your service
To all of us working here.
Your personality and charm are evident
We all like to have you near.

McNally's job is finished here
She's finished up her task.
Her mission here complete with honors
She's going home at last.

All of us here love her so
We hate to see her leave.
We've grown so used to her sweet spirit
We all will surely grieve.

We know you'll always be the same
Wherever you may trod.
The love you have for fellow man
And always serving God.

By Frances B. Mooneyhan Jr.
2009

ELDER AND SISTER DENNEY
(Leaving)

Departure time is here once more
Two more of our finest are leaving.
The departure of both will cause a big void
And cause us all very much grieving.

Brother and Sister are leaving for home.
We will sure miss all that they do.
Their duties were many, we sure loved the Denneys.
They fit so well in our crew.

Both of them are quiet and reserved
Not much was heard of each one.
But the service they gave to the Cons Lab
Will be remembered for years to come.

He's our zone leader, our guide and our friend
We trust his direction and advise.
His loyalty and love come from above
And couldn't be changed at any price.

Good luck to you both, I know you'll do great
In your service where ever you go.
We love you both and wish you the best
You've been a pleasure to know.

By Frances B. Mooneyhan Jr.
2009

ELDER AND SISTER ELDRIDGE
(Are Heading Home)

Elder and Sister Eldridge are heading home
Now their mission here is through.
They are going to have such fun
As old friendships they renew.

As you leave our lab
Your presence will be missed.
You have brought a special spirit
With your hard work and your wit.

May health and strength return to you
Each and every day.
And may God's tender mercies
Be with you on your way.

By Francis B. Mooneyhan Jr.
2009

ELDER AND SISTER ELMER
(Leaving)

Elder and Sister Elmer
Will be leaving soon for home
Leaving here a vacancy
A lot of jobs and tasks alone.

They both worked very quietly
Along with all the rest
Giving the Conservation Lab
The greatest and the best.

Time wasn't for them a problem
Starting early, working late
Some of these are qualities
We all appreciate.

They both love the Lord so much
And serve their mission well
The caliber of each missionary
By their actions you can tell.

Though you'll be sorely missed by all
Best wishes from the crew
We wish the best as you depart
And bid to you adieu.

By Francis B. Mooncyhan Jr.
2009

BROWN'S FAREWELL

I cannot tell the great impact
Your leaving has on us.
The work you've done—for everyone
Without a care or fuss.

Elder Brown and Sister Brown
You're always in our heart.
When you go home—we're left alone
Hate to see you both depart.

Your work here was very dear
Your company such a pleasure
When you leave—we sure will grieve
But your friendship we will treasure.

Our loss is another's gain
Where ever you may be
And your work there—as it was here
Will be done happily

We say farewell, but not goodbye
I'm sure we'll meet once more
If not in this life, then another
Upon another shore.

By Francis B. Mooneyhan Jr.
September 8, 2008

Eduardo's Farewell

Promotion comes to those deserving
Eduardo's no exception.
His name came up when needs arose
And came into conception.

His talents met—yea even exceeded.
The needs for that position
We'll try to make it easy for him
When he makes the transition.

The one in our group that's leaving
Whose name is Eduardo
Leaves behind us all grieving.
We hate to see us go.

There's a vacuum when he leaves
Many talents with him goes
The impact that he had on us
No one ever knows.

Vast knowledge of the lab and crew
And ability to repair
All equiptment used inside
Or used most anywhere

Although we'll miss you when you're gone
Our loss is another's gain.
We wish you much success out there.
Please visit us again.

By Francis B. Mooneyhan Jr.
October 2008

DONKERSGOED FAREWELL

What a sad day for the Conservation Lab
To stay we wish he would
We're losing one of the finest to serve
Our dear Elder Donkergoed.

Oh what a craftsman, he sure is great
Makes anything we need
You name it, he can do it
To make our lab succeed.

He has a great heart and winning smile
Personality great has he
Just quietly does his work each day
And eagerly helps you and me.

Oh how we'll miss this great friend
We've grown to love so much
Wherever you go, we hope you know
We hope you'll keep in touch.

By Francis B. Mooneyhan Jr.
2009

DIAMONDS FAREWELL

Even though you come part time
Full time efforts we did get
Your full and loyal service
We'll never soon forget.

You both work hard to ease our load
No grumbling did we hear
And when another task was given
Your help was always near.

We've come to love you both so much
We hate to see you go
Your love and friendship means a lot
As both of you well know

May God bless you on your next mission
As we know you will be serving
God loves you for the work you do
His blessings you're deserving.

By Francis B. Mooneyhan Jr.
2009

RANVEIG—THE GREAT ONE
(Farewell)

A lot of people from this lab
Have left—there's quite a list
But none that's left with such an
impact
As Ranveig—she surely will be
missed

Retirement comes to all of us
And she is no exception.
She worked for many years in here
Until she reached perfection

That she did on every job
She really knew them all
On procedures to mend the books
She's the best we can recall.

In the training she would excel
When new missionaries would arrive
To mend, binding and do repairs
In excellence she did strive.

She could do another's job
And do it as well as they.
Do it perfectly every time.
For that was Ranveig's way.

We'll miss her when she leaves.
We'll miss her dear sweet face.
The main problem that we'll have
Is someone to take her place.

By Francis B. Mooneyhan Jr.
November 2008

OF ALL THE THINGS WE'VE EVER DONE

Of all the things we've ever done
To serve with you has been such fun.
Enjoyed your friendship, love and mirth
Our associations of greatest worth

All of this has meant so much
We truly then must keep in touch
I hate to see this good year-end
We never want to lose a friend.

So where ever you go remember me
And we certainly shall remember thee
Write or call, email or visit
That's not too hard to do, now is it?

Nothing else could be any finer
Than have you visit South Carolina
To show you all how much we care
Would thrill our hearts to have you there.

By Francis B. Mooneyhan Jr.
March 2009

Final Lab Farewell

The last Lab poem I'll write this year
Is to all of you I hold so dear

The time's too short to tell each one
Your impact on my heart has done

Your kind sweet spirit his year has brought
Much more to me than you have thought

I'll always remember each one of you
No matter where I go or what I do

Although I'll return to South Carolina
I'll never meet a group any finer.

By Francis B. Mooneyhan Jr.
April 14, 2009

MISSION FAREWELL

Been to a lot of places
Done a lot of things
But none to bring contentment
That serving God can bring

This year has been the greatest
To serve with each of you
I can't believe it's ending
And my tour of duty's through

It breaks my heart to leave you all
No group could be any finer
But there are other calls for me
Way back in South Carolina

With those sweet magnolia blossoms
And that good old southern drawl
A southern hospitality saying
Come down to see us now ya'all

By Francis B. Mooneyhan Jr.
March 9, 2009

MISSION DEPARTURE

Well folks, it's time for my departure
I've been here for one full year
And so the time for leaving you
Is rapidly drawing near.

There's no way I can tell you
How much you've meant to me
This love for you I'll carry
Throughout eternity

We are all God's children
He loves us very much.
So much so, we keep this bond
And always stay in touch.

I'll care for you so very much
Where ever you abide
If again I don't see you on this earth
I'll see you on the other side.

By Francis B. Mooneyhan Jr.
April 2-2009

MISCELLANOUS

The Way We view Things
Speak Kindly To Others
Don't Bite the Hand
Take Time To Smell The Flowers
Old Folks
The Doctor's Office
The waiting Room
A Doctor's Visit
Learning Is Fun
Becoming Wiser
Darkness-Light
Earth Experience
Years Supply
Speaking In Church
You'll See Him Again
Getting Older
Nothing
Response to Veterans Letters
Running out of Tomorrows

THE WAY WE VIEW THINGS

What kind of people lived
In the place where you came from?
They were mostly bad people
They acted really dumb.

Another was asked
Was that your case too?
What kind of people
Was attracted to you?

They were really great people
And I admit, I must grieve
To tell you the truth
I hated to leave.

So what is the difference
In the way we see things?
Whatever we're seeking
Are the things that life brings

So hold up your chin
And look for the best
You'll find you're better off
Than most of the rest.

By Francis B. Mooneyhan

July 28, 2008

Speak Kindly To Others

Be careful how you speak to others
And run down their good name.
Someday, somewhere there'll be some
To you may do the same.

What you cast upon the waters,
Will all come back to you.
Be careful how you cast the stone
And what you say and do.

Especially in display of kinship
For in their influence you have part.
To them – they should be special.
Be closer to your heart.

So if there are imperfections
Remember you must share.
For you alone had their protection
And training for their care.

Speak no ill of anyone
Especially the weak
Remember that the Lord has said
To turn the other cheek.

To be like Christ, we must forgive
And pardon everyone
If we want to be forgiven
By the Father and the Son.

So be careful what you say
For words can really hurt.
Kind words would be much better
Than unkind in the dirt.

When you speak unkind of others
The Father looks the same of you.
You must love and build up others
And Christ will also to you do.

You say you love the Father
And proud to be His son.
You need your sons to feel the same.
You're not the only one.

Fathers everywhere take pride
In families that they rear.
They educate and train them
And always want them near.

Unkind words can drive a wedge
And send them far away.
If you want them close forever
Be careful what you say.

By Frances B. Mooneyhan Jr.
October 2008

Don't Bite The Hand That Feeds You

Don't bite the hand that feeds you
As the saying goes.
Just where this saying came from
It seems that no one knows.

It seems so true with wife and kids
And even Jesus Christ
We're always at our worse with them
Never thinking twice

Frustrations taken out on them
They get blamed for everything.
All the wrongs, but not the good
That only they can bring.

Jesus gives us everything
Family, health and life
We always call on Him
With troubles or with strife

He blesses us with health and strength
And food upon our table
Lifts us when we're feeling blue
And sees that we're always able

Provides us another chance
That we can live forever
Without the love of Jesus Christ
Our chances would be never.

He gives us all a chance to live
With Him forever more
With family, friends and loved ones too
He closes up death's door.

He gives the beauties of this earth
With all the sights and sounds
For our enjoyment, care and use
His love for us abounds.

Our earthly needs, He too supplies
For our needs and our enjoyment
Educations, shelter, food and such
And grants us good employment.

When things go right – we soon forget
From whence our source above
We're all wrapped up in our joy
And forget about His love.

Attend ballgames don't go to church
Our tithes are spent for pleasure.
No home evening for the kids
So they can find pure treasure.

We cut ourselves off from the Lord
Though hard as He may try
To help us turn our life around
Before we have to die.

For only in this life do we show
Our deeds by what we do
Accept the good things given to us
Don't bite the hand that's feeding you.

By Francis B. Mooneyhan Jr.
October 2008

TAKE TIME TO SMELL THE FLOWERS

Often, we don't take the time
To enjoy the things that's ours
We need to slow down just a bit-
Take time to smell the flowers

There's beauty all around us
In every step we take.
We need to take time from hurrying,
From duties take a break.

God made this world for all our needs,
With beauties all around.
What we should do is stop and look
To find the sights and sounds.

Each flower here is different
In detail and each shape.
Aromas that we get from them
Arouse us with the smells they make

The bees are aware of flowers.
From them they make what's sweet.
Don't waste the beauties that abound
Growing all around your feet.

So don't let gifts to you slide by.
His love and grace are ours.
Be cognizant of all around you.
Take time to smell the flowers.

By Francis B. Mooneyhan
August 13, 2008

Old Folks

There's lots of "Old Folks"
Everywhere you go
Their number's slowly creeping up
As you well may know.

You would think as they get older
They have but one desire
To forget the daily work
Just sit back and retire.

A lot of them are wising up.
They're wanting something more.
Something down inside of them
Is pushing from the core.

It's God's Spirit calling them
An urge to call them home.
He has for them a better place
And they never more need roam.

They've used up all their better years
In searching for wealth and fame.
Doing everything they can
To build a famous name.

Later on their values change.
They find they're not so clever.
They know that man was put on earth
But not to live forever.

That being true, what can we do?
The thoughts are real perplexing.
Where from, why here,
When will we go?
That's a real good Question

In searching for some answers,
Some changes must be made.
No longer can we worldly be
And just sit in the shade.

God requires us all to work.
Our rewards depend on this.
If we want to live with him
In eternal bliss.

So being wise from all his years,
Putting 2 and 2 together
He knows that we must get to work
To live with Him forever.

So laden down with many ails
And not in good condition,
He wants to get in good with God,
So he decides to serve a mission.

Lay not your treasures up on earth,
Where thieves break in and steal.
But lay up treasures in God's kingdom.
Then _your_ reward, He will reveal.

By Francis B. Mooneyhan Jr.
October 2008

In The Doctor's Office

Sitting in the doctors office
Talking to the sick
Hoping my turn with him is soon
So I can get out quick.

Aches and pains that others have
Never dawn on you
Until you sit and talk with them
Then yours are just a few.

When you think that you have troubles
There're others worse off than you
And if you stop awhile and think
You could have had them too.

Be thankful for the days you have
When things are not too bad
There are many others worse off than you
With problems you've never had.

So why am I here, I ask myself
I didn't slip or fall
Don't have pneumonia or the flu
I feel pretty well after all.

By Francis B. Mooneyhan Jr.
September 2008

THE WAITING ROOM

Sitting in the waiting room
With nothing else to do
Waiting for my turn to come
Hoping I don't get the flu

Everyone has problems now
Most of us can't cope
With the troubles we all have
Some are losing hope.

Things we do and things we eat
Are causing many woes
Just what will happen next
It seems that no one knows.

Whatever comes we must be ready
Not ever thinking twice
Because we all would like
Someday to live with Christ

By Francis B. Mooneyhan Jr.
January 14, 2009

DOCTORS VISIT

You go to see the doctor
To refill a prescription.
Two hours later he comes in
To check on your condition.

Before he does, his nurse is first
It really makes her day.
She puts you up upon the scales
To see how much you weigh.

Another nurse comes in and smiles
Comes tornado or a flood
Before you leave the office
They're going to get your blood.

You wonder if you have enough
With all the vials and cups.
She squeezes, pats and punches
Until she fills them up.

Your temperature is taken
Your pulse, blood pressure too.
They look at you real funny
As if you have the flu.

Just for a precaution
You should get an injection
After all, to play it safe
So you don't get infections.

What about tuberculosis?
The measles or the mumps?
They then check you all over
To see if they find lumps.

You're convinced that viruses
Are going all around
And that you need protection
Before you leave this town.

Before you leave you have several shots.
Now, you really *are* in pain.
You only came to see the Doc
Because of a bad migraine.

By Francis B. Mooneyhan Jr.

Learning is Fun

(Mrs. Bliss' 1st grade class)

We are sharp
We are fast
We are Mrs. Bliss'
1st grade class

(Chorus)
Learning is fun
Learning is fun
Learning is fun
For everyone

Oh what joy
Oh what fun
Being together
So we can learn

(Chorus)

Learning to count
Learning to read
Put it together
So we'll succeed

(Chorus)

All about animals
In the zoo
All about people
Just like you

(Chorus)

Learn about country
Learn about town
Learn about everything
All around

(Chorus)
Sing with joy
And clapping hands
Teaching helps us
To understand

(Chorus)

By Frank Mooneyhan Jr.
November 2008

BECOMING WISER

As you age and become much older
You find you get less bolder.

Not as fearless, rude or rowdy
Enjoy the sunshine, though less cloudy

When you're young, you feel so clever
Think that you will live forever

But that's not true, as you will see
You live not longer than the tree.

The ones you know have come and gone
And now you're left here all alone.

Sometimes there's faith, sometimes there's doubt
You wonder what life's all about.

You know your fate is sealed out there
Just don't know exactly where

Our life is written day by day
The things we do—the things we say

We put together the things we learn
With Christ we live—without Him burn.

We hope our fate we can arrange
And think real soon to make a change

Now's the time to change, my friend
Don't wait until the very end.

To be forgiven and live with Him
Or find your chances very dim

So wise up now and live forever
That way you don't need to be so clever.

It's so easy to do what's right
Not have to worry day and night

And all of this by being wise
To live with Christ in Paradise

By Francis B. Mooneyhan Jr.- January 1, 2009

DARKNESS

Some folks like the darkness
Because there's no light
The absence of sunlight
The term we call night.

Some like it for sleeping
Some like it for fun
Some like it to tell
When the day's work is done.

Some use it for hiding
To cover their sins
Shutting out Christ
So He can't enter in.

In Satan there's darkness
In him there's _no_ light
It doesn't make any difference
If it's daylight or night.

So there's good and bad
In the things that we choose
Make sure it's the right choice
That way you don't loose.

LIGHT

Where does light come from?
Some really don't know.
I think that I can tell
For the bible tells me so.

The light is in Christ
He's the light of the world.
In all that he does
The truth will unfurl

The truth is also light
That comes from Him
And He can make it shine
In us, deep down within.

When you keep his
commandments
You're the light of Christ
And then trough the Savior
You're also the light.

By Francis B. Mooneyhan
2008

EARTH EXPERIENCE

We're put on Earth to gain experience
To see what life's about
To know first hand just how it feels
Or try to figure it out.

Sometimes with pain and sickness
Helps us to know how others feel
Often the problems are our own
To see if we will kneel.

To learn of earth and skies and seas
Or underneath the earth
To absorb experiences we have each day
To see what life is worth.

We need to hear and see and feel
To find out why we're here.
Someday we're going back to our God.
These experiences will be dear.

So don't begrudge unhappy days
When things don't go your way
Remember they're just for our good
And they were planned that way.

By Francis B. Mooneyhan
February 10, 2009

YEARS SUPPLY

For years we've heard the prophet's cry
For us to have a year's supply

We listened not, a deaf ear turned
It seems that we have never learned.

We put things off, hope for the best
Acting like most of the rest.

Though we're not mired up in the mud
It wasn't raining before the flood.

Prepare we must along each day
Or disaster may come our way.

Without a warning or a call
Someday could be our great downfall.

We've been warned, deny we durst
Or else our family will starve and thirst.

Save a little week by week
Keeps us prepared for what we seek.

Take care of family and not deny
To be prepared with our years supply

When food is gone and you are cold
You cannot say you were not told.

By Francis B. Mooneyhan Jr.
February 9, 2009

SPEAKING IN CHURCH

I was assigned to speak in church
That's really quite a task.
I'm not too good at doing this
I wish they hadn't asked.

Too many topics from which to choose
And any one will do.
We need the knowledge from each talk
Because they all are true.

Convincing others to make a change
In the way they live each day
To make a change for Jesus Christ
For He's the only way.

But mine is not to turn them down
Just do the best I can
Always carry the spirit there
To help my fellow man.

By Francis B. Mooneyhan Jr.
April 3 2009

YOU'LL SEE HIM AGAIN

Gina, don't worry about Jake
For he is in a better place
The good news is for you
Again you'll see his face.

God also knows just how you feel
He also sacrificed a Son
At the cross on Calvary
For you and everyone

Christ did it because He loves us
He suffered grief and pain
So we'd never be alone
And be together once again

We are all His children
Christ loves like you and I
Sorrow fills His heart like yours
Whenever we pass Him by.

So trust in Christ with all your heart
Your pains, He'll bear for you.
Your sorrows will be lightened
Where ever you go or what you do.

He wants us all at home with Him
For all to celebrate
There are loved ones waiting
To see us and can hardly wait.

So lean on Christ and keep His laws
And He will share your pain.
Your days of sorrow will be short
For you *will be* with Jake again.

By Francis B. Mooneyhan Jr.
May 12-2009

164

GETTING OLDER

On April the tenth
I'll be seventy-nine.
Some days aren't too good.
Some days I feel fine.

So what can you expect
For a man of my age
Some days of being flippant
Some days an sold sage

Some days I can function
Some days I cannot
Some days I remember
Some things I forgot

It's nice to be young
Not too bad to be old
It's nice to be warm
A place to come in from the cold

It's nice to have children
And I love all seven
They're all very nice
On earth, they're my Heaven

A good wife that loves me
And stays by my side
I love her more now
Than when a young bride

And grandchildren too
Don't leave any of them out
At my age, I can dream
That's what life's all about

On my life's journey
Most conditions I've met
But in spite of it all
Some things I forget.

That's part of getting older
Nothing's ever the same
I'll just take what I get
I'll not be 20 again.

So stick with me family
Let's share love together
The love that we share
Will be with us forever.

By Frances B. Mooneyhan Jr.
March 2010

When will we go? That's a real good question

NOTHING

I love to write poetry though I'm not very good
I'd like to do better—I sure wish I could.

I try each day with eager and zest
To do a better job and be at my best

I've run out of topics to be writing about
And other things that could just do without

So with nothing to write about—that's a good subject too
Since I don't have anything else to do

So if nothing is nothing there's nothing to care
You don't even have to be thinking it's there

If I write about nothing then people won't care
If there's nothing to read then there's nothing there

Nothing to see or nothing to read
Nothing to care about if you don't succeed

Void of content—void of text
No need to worry about what's coming next

I'm so glad I've chosen nothing this time
Who cares if there's anything nothing will rhyme.

By Francis B. Mooneyhan Jr.
November 2009

RESPONSE TO VETERAN LETTERS

Got the letters sent from you
I'm proud of what you try to do
Lift up the spirits of service men
You've started on a real good trend.

All of you are learning fast
I'm glad you're in Mrs. Bliss' class
Patriotism taught in school
Follows like a Golden Rule

You learn of country and freedom too
All of this means much to you
In a great country you can be proud
Things you do stand out from the crowd

I'm glad I'm a veteran and proud of you
I really love our Red White and Blue
May our country always be free
We can do it—you and me

It means a lot you didn't forget
You make us proud to be a Vet.

By Francis B. Mooneyhan
November 14, 2010

RUNNING OUT OF TOMORROWS

As I sit here, I regret to my great sorrow
I've just about run out of tomorrows.

I'm, feeble and old and turning grey,
Troubles piling up on me every day.

My vision is going, my hearing too.
There's not much left that I can do.

Where are the years when I was my best
Full of vim, vigor and zest.

As I sit here and think, <u>Tomorrow's not here</u>"
I still have today, and <u>to me</u> that's so dear.

My family and love ones I have all around.
The sound of their laughter, how I love that sound.

Tho I'm almost out of tomorrows, I still have today
To have and enjoy, I like it better that way.

By Francis B. Mooneyhan Jr.
July 21, 2011

ODE TO OTHERS

Air Guard Wives
Ode Elder Denney
Sister Denney
Clyde Black Tribute
Two Special Missionaries
Ode to the McAtees
Two Special Home Teachers
Ode to Elder Davis
Ode To Scarlett
Thanks Camden Ward
Homecoming Gift
Ode to Elizabeth
Ode to Eddie
My Good Neighbor

Air Guard Wives

Here's to the ones we left behind
So sweet, so wonderful and fine

Here's to the children and the wives
Whose men were taken from their lives

To form together in a band
And go to some far unknown land.

For just how long we didn't know
Or for what reason we must go.

But go we did with saddened hearts
To leave our wives and dear sweethearts.

To carry on where once we did
To run the house and raise the kids

Installments due and bills to pay
More troubles pile up every day.

The washer's broke, the faucet leaks
Their nerves are building to a peak.

But still they carry on each day
Trying to stretch our little pay.

A toast to loved ones sweet and kind
Here's to the ones we left behind.

Bu Francis B. Mooneyhan
1961

170

ODE ELDER DENNEY

Lots of things in life are hard
To describe them, trials a plenty
That's the way I fell right now
About co-worker, Elder Denney

Of all the nice things to be said
I'm certainly not adept
Although they need to be brought out
He wouldn't speak of self.

Humble, gentle, kind and thoughtful
That way to every one
The way we all need to re-act
He emulates the Son.

It's been a pleasure all year long
To know and work with him.
And all the lab crew feels the same
They've felt his love for them.

We'll surely miss him when he leaves
We'll miss his smiling face.
Replacement becomes a daunting task
For another to take his place.

By Francis B. Mooneyhan Jr.
April 2009

SISTER DENNEY

There's a missionary sister in our lab.
Her name is Sister Denny.
She's been blessed with many gifts
Like kindness and patience a plenty.

She sits there so sweetly with a smile on her face.
When I bring her my poems for her blessing
She reads every one—though I know it's no fun.
She never gives me a redressing.

She's that way—to those around her each day
Shows kindness to everyone
She makes us feel good—like everyone should
We feel better when the day's work is done.

By Francis B. Mooneyhan Jr.
June 9, 2008

CLYDE BLACK TRIBUTE

My name is Francis Mooneyhan
A happy life I've had
All because I've found the Lord
And put away the bad

I joined the church in '54.
In the south the church was small.
I met a man who towered great
His spiritual height was tall.

The name they call him is Clyde Black.
He has served in all positions
From teacher, bishoprics, stake president too
And even Temple and presidency missions

He's been a friend to all he knew
Throughout his church career
A spiritual giant and guiding light
To all of them so dear

He's been my example from baptism date
To a mission I'm now serving
I'm sure he's loved by the Lord and others
Great blessings he's deserving.

A pioneer in time of need
I n building faith we lack
A worthy son that Jesus loves
Is our dear President Black

Ninety years he's been on earth
To bless the ones he loves
Now we give him our respect
Along with those above

By Francis B. Mooneyhan Jr.
January 29, 2009

TWO SPECIAL MISSIONARIES

When you go on a mission you're given a task
To teach or lighten the load of man
Some fit in well to accomplish this
In doing the best they can.

Others are blessed with great talents
Exceeding that of many
This goes for two special missionaries,
Doctor Hansen and Sister Matheney.

The potential is there to treat many souls
The task is great as can be
Some will be sent to special doctors
But to some of them, it will be free.

Most sick missionaries are well up in age
With lots of ills, that's for sure
Dr. Hansen and Nurse Matheney are trying hard
To help them through kindness and cure.

There's not much time to take a break
Or breathing a sigh of relief
Their time's taken up 8 hours a day
Trying to ease many others of grief.

By Francis B. Mooneyhan Jr.

ODE TO THE McATEES

The McAtees are leaving
And we sure will be grieving.
They helped us all out a lot.
Even helped with the labels
When I was unable
To catch up with the load that I got.

They were both standing tall
As they assisted us all
In our labors throughout the shop.
They had energy galore
And they wanted to do more.
Their labors never did stop.

Multi-talented are they
And they've shown it each day
By the things they did for each one.
The love for their friends
In the lab never ends
As they leave when the day's work is
done.

The love for their God
And the path here they've trod
Will impress everyone I know
The example they've set
Is to be equaled yet
In their journeys where 'ere they go.

We'll miss their good laughter
When they leave us after
The end of the month to go home
Though he'll be somewhere
In his old rocking chair
I'll certainly not be here alone.

I'll have plenty to do
With a sweet loving crew
As my time will come soon enough.
But in my dismay
I know that someday
My separation day
Will also really be tough!

By Francis B. Mooneyhan Jr.
November 6 2008

175

SPECIAL HOME TEACHERS

My home teachers are the Claysens
And they are good as gold
Get around with zeal and zest
For they are not too old.

Elder Claysen's always available
For that is just his way
Does all for us that he can do
To help me make the day

Helps me through the priesthood
As often I did seek
Kept me steady on the job
For I used it week by week

Faithful home teachers, kind and serving
Visiting us each month
As we understood the gospel
Their messages would triumph

Always around to help in need
Remembering special dates
Fulfill their duties as home teachers
To see that nothing waits

A ride each Monday to devotional
I couldn't walk that far.
The walk up hill would strain my heart
So they carried me by car.

They've been so kind in every way
Assignment secondary
Just serving God the way they should
And being good missionaries

When we leave this mission
We'll miss them very much
Their friendship means a lot to us
We hope to keep in touch

If not this life, then surely next
Pure love never ends.
God provides a way for us
To forever be with friends.

By Francis B. Mooneyhan Jr.
April 16. 2009

ODE TO ELDER DAVIS

Ode to a great missionary
Robin Davis is his name.
No claim of being perfect
Or climbing to great fame

Other talents he possesses
That of helping people
He stands out great in this regard
Like a church with a shiny steeple

He gives of time to others
Not thinking of his own
In the genealogy library
Or even in his home

Service is the greatest gift
Required of God to all
And those who don't give it
God in Heaven will not call.

So thanks we give to Elder Davis
For assistance that he gives
We'll be thankful for all he's doing
For as long as we shall live

Father is thankful to all His servants
Who give, not thinking twice
And He embraces them in Heaven
To live with Him and Christ

By Francis B. Mooneyhan Jr.
April 17, 2009

ODE TO SCARLETT

I've read the life story
Of Scarlett (Watson) Ange
A wonderful nice person
And that surely won't change

She's the life of the party
Or with one-on-one
Nice to be around her
Because she's so much fun

Intelligent and witty
With so much to say
She loves being with family
Each and every day

I've known her a long time
Feel part of the clan
I married a Watson
Now she's a Mooneyhan

Your life story is not over
I'm sure you realize
You'll have more to add later
Before Paradise

By Francis B. Mooneyhan Jr.
November 28, 2009

THANKS CAMDEN WARD

(Christmas Greeting)

Though we're far away from you
Your kindness reached out here.
We're thankful for the cards you sent.
We hold them very dear.

Your love and friendship means a lot
Where ever we may go
Thanks so much for taking time
Just wanted you to know

We hope you all are doing well
And filled with love and cheer.
May joy and peace be with each one
All throughout the year.

The peace and joy that Christ can bring
To each and every heart
Can make this Christmas great for you
And give the New Year a great start.

By Francis B. Mooneyhan Jr.
December 2008

HOMECOMING GIFT

Thanks so much to all of you
For our homecoming you did do

Your own desires and needs did douse
So you could go and clean our house.

Our expectation didn't plan
For us to get a helping hand.

Your love for us sincerely shows
As ours for you forever grows

Thanks again for that great favor.
I'm sure your love will please our Savior.

By Francis B. Mooneyhan Jr.
April 22, 2009

ODE TO ELIZABETH

Ode to Elizabeth
The last of my seven
This sweet gal is my best pal
Was sent to me from Heaven

Wonderful sweet and loving daughter
I love with all my heart
A loving mind and oh so kind
And has been from the start

She teaches school to lots of tots
And tries to help their day
All through her trial—she still can smile
She functions best that way

She loves all children large and small
Has patience just like Job
Throughout the day she finds a way
No matter what the load

She knows the joys that children bring
To her most every day
Knowing this, sweet Mrs. Bliss
Wants children sent her way

She pleads with God to honor her
To start a family
And so each day she pleads and prays
That it real soon shall be

Suddenly the answer came
That day was like no other
The Father's will to give a thrill
She was going to be a mother!

Oh what a day to celebrate
To a mother soon to be
Mom and Dad sure was glad
To start their family

Rearing children is a real tough job
Takes patience and gives much stress
But what a joy—a girl and boy
Can lives of families bless

ODE TO EDDIE

Congratulation, Eddie, you're a teacher 1st class
It's such a pleasure to be in your class.

You teach by the spirit, which you impart to us all.
All through the class your countenance never falls.

The material for your class, you check more than twice.
You want to make sure it magnifies Christ.

You do a great job making us feel good.
You make it interesting as a good teacher should.

You're a great example of a Latter-Day Saint.
You can do many things that other people can't.

Your example of a teacher leaves others in the dust.
In preparing your lesson, you do what you must.

There's no preparation that you leave behind.
All of this indicates a great spiritual mind.

Keep up the good work, it's not all in vain.
The worth of your labor will meet you again.

By Francis B. Mooneyhan Jr.
June 12, 2011

MY GOOD NEIGHBOR

I have a good neighbor who lives next door.
A better neighbor, I couldn't ask for more.

Always around in time of need
trying to do his daily good deed.

His Christian demeanor grows every day.
The love of Christ makes him that way.

Love of family, hard working too
willing to help me and you.

Whatever the task, he gets the job done.
Too hot or too cold, he always has fun.

I'm feeble and old and can't mow my lawn
But he's cutting my grass right after dawn.

Whatever my need, he's always around.
I never remember him letting me down.

Love your neighbor the good book reads
He puts into action by all his good deeds.

By Francis B. Mooneyhan Jr.
July 25, 2011

PERSONAL

A Short Life Sketch
Required Attention
Trials, Trials, Trials
Worst and Best Year
Priesthood Blessings
My Valentine Miracle
Testimony

   (Questions)
What Can I Do?
Wondering Why?
Why?
Why Me Lord
Where do you Fit In?

A SHORT LIFE SKETCH

I'll attempt to write some history
Of my childhood growing up
Some may be in detail
And some might be abrupt

I was born early in the 30's
And grew up on a farm
Most of the time was working
Not much time for charm

The time was during the depression
And we were poor like all
The things that I remember most
Was picking cotton in the fall

Our vocation was Share Cropping
Not much to make a living
We seemed to get along alright
In all of our misgiving

I couldn't start to school on time
'Till the crops were gathered in
We had to walk to school barefooted
To save the shoes and toughen skin

I was number one in line
Sara Lou and Annie Lee
The children from mother one
Only made it up to three

Help was needed as you can see
For I was only five
Someone else must come and help
If we were to survive

Another family started
It really wasn't bad
We had to make a living
As we were all each other had.

As I recall we moved a lot
From place to place we'd roam
Trying to find a place to work
And trying to find a home

As time went on and things improved
We went our separate ways
Trying to make a better life
Improve our later days

I enlisted in the Air Force
With nothing else to do
Decided it was time for me
To learn a skill or two

After that Carolina bound
Never should have tarried
Not too long I settled down
Decided to get married

A great decision in my life
I married Kathleen.
More happiness than I've ever had
My life became serene.

She had a strong influence on me
Helped me to join the church
I then accepted Jesus Christ
And ended my long search

Now there's hope for family and me
For us to live together
For all eternity
Forever and forever

So goes the history of Francis B
Not completed as of yet
More children add from my children
Will get much better, I'll bet

By Francis B. Mooneyhan Jr.
January 2, 2009

REQUIRED ATTENTION

It seems that each and every week
A need for blessings do I seek.

I have so many ills and aches
That many blessings for me it takes.

Seems I'm never feeling fine
It takes so much of FATHER'S time.

Although He comes when ever I call
I hate to call on Him at all.

He heals us as He said He would
When calling on His great priesthood.

Some have the gift to heal the sick.
Some have the gift to be healed quick.

Whatever the case, I'm glad He's there
To reach Him all I need is prayer.

Although my needs are great each day
He always hears me when I pray.

By Francis B. Mooneyhan
February 23, 2009

TRIALS TRIALS TRIALS

It started out when I first arrived
With problems not anticipated.
Had trouble walking to work and back.
I wasn't acclimated.

As soon as I got over that
My knees and hips, more pain.
It wasn't hard to figure out
I needed prayer again.

We figured out the troubles there
To alarm and to excite us.
The reasons I could hardly move
Was due to arthritis.

That wasn't all, there's more to come
From an injury long ago
With the task I had at work
Caused another injury to show.

Faith and prayer once more did come
To solve this trial for me
In spite of all I'd been through
I wasn't trouble free.

June came, the worst month of my life
And I was racked with pain again.
Inflammation that earlier blinded me
Was at my door again.

He always answers when I ask.
He hasn't failed me yet.
I was told that all my troubles
Started in my neck.

Where the nerve came through my spine
And because of degeneration
It became to be inflamed
That caused my inflammation.

I couldn't sleep in bed or chair.
The nerve I'd agitate
Once again the spirit said
Adjustments I must take.

I was told to use a pillow
Around my neck to keep.
Keeps it straight, not falling over
So I could get some sleep.

So now I sleep in a chair
At 45 degrees.
A pillow around my neck and chest
So now I sleep with ease.

They called in an orthopedic specialist.
I told her of my dream and plight.
She told me all of this was true.
The Spirit told me right.

MRI's and X-rays
Confirmed a severe Stenosis.
Once again the Spirit's right
In giving His dignosis.

Don't under estimate your Father
He loves you very much.
He's always patiently waiting
For us to get in touch.

He didn't say that it would be easy
As we journey on our way.
But He's always there to lift us up
Each and every day.

I went to see another specialist
On October twenty nine.
To see if they could operate
Or would I be just fine?

An answer back from the MRI
There's nothing he can do
To help me out and ease my pain
On my own I must pull through

Decision made to keep it simple
Just nothing at this time
Hoping that through faith and fasting
I could make it out just fine.

So for now that's what I'm doing
Holding out 'till I get home
No matter what the outcome
Jesus never leaves me on my own.

Got a blessing from the Priesthood
Now I'm home and at this time
Didn't need an operation
God has healed me, now I'm fine.

By Francis B. Mooneyhan – March 21, 2009

Worst and Best Year

Health in 2008 was not too good.
It started before my mission.
Didn't know how I would fare
When making my transition.

One month went by and all went well.
I thought my troubles done.
But not the case, I soon found out
For they had just begun.

June, the worst month of my life,
I ached with pain all over
Couldn't use my arms and hands
Pain mostly in my shoulder.

From that start, a mighty change
Would take place in my life
The spiritual side of me would grow
Because of Jesus Christ.

Being more thoughtful for all my blessings
Having sympathy for all the sick
Seeing others with appreciation
And trying not to judge too quick.

More love for wife and those around me
More patience and charity I have found
As I've put this into practice
More peace and joy I've seen abound.

I'm less dependent on worldly things
I appreciate family more and more
I've learned how much I love them
And pray for them o're and o're

With all the bad, there's been much good
I've grown more spiritually this year
I wouldn't trade the experiences I've had.
They've been so wonderful and dear.

By Francis B. Mooneyhan
March 12, 2009

PRIESTHOOD BLESSING

As I awoke this morning
And slowly opened my eyes
I felt that there was something different
And then to my surprise

My pain was gone—Eureka!!!
Now I could move with ease.
It seemed that from my blessing
I was eased of my disease.

I've been plagued since the first of June
With inflammation in my shoulder.
I thought at first it was just my age
As I am getting older.

But it persisted month by month
No comfort anywhere.
I couldn't find sleep night or day
In bed or in a chair.

On Saturday September 6th
I could hardly move about.
The need of help to relieve this pain
Or comfort do without.

I called upon the Priesthood
The best help I could find.
I knew that God could help me
And ease my worried mind.

As soon as the blessing was over,
I rested all that day
Feeling very much better
Because that's God's own way.

Usually while sleeping over night
In a chair or in the bed
Next morning after getting up
My arms won't rise above my head.

That's why today I'm happy
And in a real good mood
To know that God still loves me
When I call on His Priesthood.

By Francis B. Mooneyhan Jr.
September 8, 2008

MY VALENTINE MIRACLE

My same old problem came back once again
And caused me once more agony and pain
Two days I was in trouble and couldn't find relief
Trying to find comfort just caused me more grief

On Valentine's Day I was really in a mess.
I couldn't get warm though I tried my best.
The inflammation that had been so bad in my shoulder
Suddenly again I was hurting all over.

Hard chills I was having most of the day.
It was hard to keep warm though I tried every way.
Three blankets I used along with a down vest
I found that these worked out for the best.

Our home teachers had promised us most of the week
To take us both out for a valentine treat.
They both came early—I was reluctant to go.
I couldn't go in my condition, so I told them no.

A blessing was in order to get me moving
So kitty and I not a good meal would be loosing
With the priesthood blessing, I trusted the Lord.
I know when He promises, He keeps his word.

I was promised in the blessing I would be ok
And soon I'd have a much better day.
An hour later I was feeling just fine
And ready to enjoy my gift valentine.

From 7 'till 12 my pain is still gone
And I'm praising the Lord as I sit here alone.
I'm always amazed at the love Christ has for me.
When I call on the priesthood, He sets my pain free.

By Francis B, Mooneyhan Jr.
February 14, 2009

MY TESTIMONY

I have a testimony.
It burns within my heart.
The day that I was baptized
Is when it got its start.

I testify of Jesus Christ,
The Father and the Holy Ghost
Ever concerning for our welfare
Care for us the very most.

I know that Joseph was a prophet
For us in latter days
To learn of Christ and all his teaching
To live by all His love and ways.

I know that Christ is waiting
For us to keep in touch
So he can answer all our needs
Because he loves us very much.

By Francis B. Mooneyhan Jr.
October 5, 2011

WHAT CAN I DO

What can I do and what can I say
To save my family and friends from Hell
Do I speak kindly and tell them the truth
Or do I rant and rave and yell?

Whatever it takes—whatever the cost
I surely must find a way
Or else the ones that I love so much
Will be lost on judgment day.

There's much more than saying that we believe
Or going to church on Sunday
We put into practice things that we learn
And start out our week on Monday.

It takes a lot more than a token of faith
Or attendance of church now and then
We must show by the actions we take
How we treat our fellow men.

The family is first in the way they're taught
By example and the gospel we teach
Prayer and home evening are part of the course
If our goal for them we'll reach.

Baptism by 8, attendance at church
And tithing we pay without doubt.
Scripture study we do to learn of our Lord
No law that He gives is left out.

The things of this world will end
And all will be lost by and by
But treasures we store and lay up in Heaven
Will be with us when we die.

Christ is fair when He comes next to judge
We will each get what we earn
Whether we rest in Heaven
Or sent with Satan to burn.

What mother or dad or friend to all
Could want more for family than this
To live together with families and loved ones
With God in eternal bliss.

Be careful, my friends, for God is not mocked.
He knows where your true treasure lies.
You're living for Christ or living for Satan
In eternal darkness or in paradise

So what can I say to further convince
That the gospel of Christ is true
The things that you feel—will finally reveal
What means the most to you.

WONDERING WHY

Why did I leave from where I lived?
When I wasn't feeling well
To go elsewhere to a far away place
Where I must then there dwell?

And why did I come to *this* mission?
Maybe to encourage or inspire
Or just to make me humble
Of those things that I require.

I never thought *much* of record keeping
Before I came out west
Maybe this is why I came
Maybe this is my test.

Without the history that's been written
Of those gone on before
All those things would be forgotten
Lost to us forever more.

I know *now* that it's my mission
To record the things I feel
Some you'll like and some you won't
Some bring sorrow—some appeal.

So I'll record and keep a journal
Of things that happen day by day
And hope that this will help you
As I happily go my way.

Things I leave for all my children
Things I hope they will save
I leave with you my testimony
And not take it to the grave.

By Francis B. Mooneyhan Jr.
2008

WHY?

Why did I leave home
With a comfortable position
To go far away
To serve on a mission?

Why leave my family
And all that I own
To go someplace else
Far away from home?

Why work 8 hours
When before I did none
And walk all the way
In the rain, snow or sun?

Why go outside
When there's 3 feet of snow
Still trudge to work
And feel the cold wind blow?

Though the questions are many
The answers are there
We love HEAVENLY FATHER
And we show Him we care.

If we believe in the scriptures
Like we say we do
We'll keep His commandments
And always be true.

What do we have here?
That will last a long time
That you can say truly
All this is mine?

All that you have
Is a gift God has loaned
You really have nothing
That's your very own.

Why ask Him why
When His saints he must use
To misuse our talents
We have no excuse.

So when the Lord calls
We don't *need* to ask why
Just give Him your best
And tell Him we'll try.

For what is the prize
If we do it *His* way
To be with our families
When comes judgment day?

By Francis B. Mooneyhan Jr.
December 9, 2008

WHY ME LORD

You send a spirit down to earth
To get a body at time of birth

Some are healthy, some are weak
But all of them are ours to keep

The last one came, oh what a shame
Never would he know his name

Cannot use his arms or legs
Can't feed himself, for speech he begs

We love him so in spite of needs
And hope somehow he soon succeeds

We worry so of needs without
Give love and help and be devout

But it's a burden for us all
He never will grow strong and tall

Why me Lord to face this task
I'm sorry but I have to ask

Fear not my child, the answer's there
For you must learn to love and care

The afflicted will always be with us
You cannot always fret and fuss

Remember Christ has suffered too
To satisfy both me and you

Your child on earth, though not adorned
Needed a body, so he was born

God accepts him as a prize
To live with Him in paradise

By Francis B. Mooneyhan Jr.
July 7, 2009

WHERE DO YOU FIT IN

Some are placed upon the Earth
For reasons yet unknown
Protected, lead about
Their life seems not their own.

Others have such terrible times
Nothing ever goes their way
Pain and sickness seems their plight
Almost every day.

Some are rich and some are poor
Some are healthy, some are sick
Some have trouble learning
While others catch on quick.

Some are strong, and some are healthy
While others are confined to bed
Some enjoy great lifestyles
Others wish that they were dead.

What's our purpose here on Earth?
And where do we fit in
Where winners and losers here abide
But some never seem to win.

Too bad we measure success on Earth
Only by man's way
You'll find that things will be much different
When we reach the judgment day

God's plan for us is not our way
He has another plan
He rewards for what's in our heart
And how we treat our fellow man.

So just be kind and do your best
Have charity for everyone
Your reward will come to you
When you're with the Father and the Son.

By Francis B. Mooneyhan Jr.
September 2008

RELIGIOUS

Reverence—An Observation
Miracle Of The Pear Tree
Devotional Time
Faith-Hope
The House Of The Lord
Miracles
Miracle Of The Gate
In The Temple
To The Uncommitted
The Sabbath
Remembering Him
God's Children
He Did It For Us
Concern for The One
Service
The Holy Ghost
Jesus Loves All Children
Giving Thanks
A Special Gift
A World For us
Tabernacle Choir
Temple Square
Effects Of Joseph's Prayer

REVERANCE—AN OBSERVATION

Today was Sunday
The day of the Lord
I came to church early
To hear of His word

I needed some comfort
For my worried mind
This is the place
I felt I could find

There were others
From all over town
Seeking for answers
Wanting them found

A sweet dear sister
With a son in Iraq
Silently praying
That he soon would be back

There were others
Whose dreams had been lost
That had given up loved ones
At a terrible cost

A repentant teenager
Sat there with a frown
Because of Saturday night
Out on the town

A myriad of faces
Of those on the pews
With worried minds
Trying to find clues

I had trouble thinking
That I can't deny
As I sat there wondering
Just why – oh why?

So I looked all around
And to my surprise
I really could not
Believe my eyes

The things that I saw
Was so very sad
When I saw what was happening
I really felt bad

Laughing and talking
Showing pictures from purses
Some were even eating
Chocolate bar Hersheys

Feeding small ones
Cereal and crackers too
Getting the crumbs
All over the pew

Young ones were running
Up and down the aisles
While their parents
Were just making smiles

Going to the bathroom
They had just gotten there
A little more training
Would seem more fair

Kids running to the stage
Mom getting them down
Hey! Daddy can help
No fooling around

To the foyer they'll take them
Since they're so hardy
But we find out there
They're having a party.

Because out there
They can let them run
After all children
Must have their fun.

Some came in late
Like they usually do
And sat down to visit
With their regular crew

REVERANCE—AN OBSERVATION

(Continued)

Friends are nice
And it's good to visit
But the chapel's
not the place is it?

I looked for reverence
But couldn't find any
The talking and noise
I found a plenty.

Some came seeking Christ
But He left right away.
He said He'd be back
On some other day

He like His house quieter
So He can attend
There are some rules and laws
That He will not bend

Weddings are quiet
With guests ushered in
Not a sound will be made
Not even the drop of a pin

Then why not for Sacrament
The most sacred of all
Christ atoned for our sins
Because of the fall

So why go to church
If not to do what they say
Be kind –be reverent
There's no other way.

Then when you need Christ
He's right by your side.
Right there forever
With you He'll abide.

As bad as it seemed
It's really not that bad.
There's lots of youth
Sitting with Mother and Dad

Lots of folks come
Week-in and week-out
Most brothers and sisters
Are really devout

We all have faith
That we're tying to mend
Bringing up the good
That's deep down within

As bad as we are
We're trying to get better.
And all of our faults
We're trying to fetter.

We're in the right place
When we go to church Sunday
We just need to remember
"It's not a Fun Day".

We go asking forgiveness
Of things we've done wrong
And hope to do better
The whole day long

The sinner – the saint
The downtrodden and blue
The noisy – the faithful
His house is for you.

As we do our best
We all are winners!
The church, a refuge for saints
A hospital for sinners!

By Frances B. Mooneyhan
Circa 2006

205

The Miracle of The Pear Tree

Maren and I have a pear tree
That tree is really great
And every year to taste it's fruit
We both can hardly wait.

Every year we have great pears
And none are ever lost
Except one year the weather changed
We had a killing frost.

The tree was white all over
With blossoms everywhere
We knew that year would be productive
With great tasting pears

Then the frost came and it turned black
And we were in despair
We knew the season would be lost
Without a single pear

Maren sure was unhappy
She wished to save the day
She wanted to know what she could do
I told her she could pray.

We went inside to our living room
Where we usually say our prayers
She asked our Heavenly Father
To give us a few pears,

We forgot about that prayer for weeks
Until to our surprise
We saw some blossoms on the tree
We couldn't believe our eyes.

It did produce some pears that year
Although just a few
No other fruit tree in our yard
Produced like they usually do

One day when they were ripe
I lifted her up high
So she could get delicious fruit
And then I asked her why.

We ask for blessings from the Lord
In faith he blesses us
We have to show our faith in Him
In Him we place our trust.

Christ said He healed ten lepers
To thank Him only one returned
That's the way we are sometimes
We go about unlearned.

I told her this in hope to teach
A lesson about Christ
She ran to thank Him for His blessings
Never thinking twice

He wants us to be thankful
So, I told her on that day
We rushed inside our living room
And she began to pray.

An innocent child was thanking God
For blessings that He sent
That's the way that we should be
So we never need repent.

By Francis B. Mooneyhan

DEVOTIONAL TIME

I hope that I'm not out of line
In the things I'm about to say
But I think we need to be more careful
In the way we start our day.

We have a special FATHER,
Who loves us very much.
He's waiting very patiently
For us to get in touch.

But how we do that puzzles Him,
Mixed signals He receives.
Our actions speak much louder
Than the words that we will breathe

At movie time we're very quiet
We don't want to miss the show.
At weddings too, we give respect
Because of those we know.

Then why not God, the Holy One?
Let's give Him our respect
Then when we ask for blessings,
He'll surely not reject.

Devotion time is to the LORD,
To show and honor Him.
We also have our leaders
And respect we owe to <u>them.</u>

We're engaged to serve our God
And really love our work.
We try our best to do our jobs,
Our duties not to shirk.

But in our zeal to start the day,
We forget what's taking place.
The meeting starts and so do we.
We've start on our pace.

We need to have devotion time
To get God in our heart
And just slow down a bit
Before we get our start.

Not stacking books or tattles tapes
Or straightening up our desks,
Computers off and listening up
To be our very best

So start the day relaxed and calm,
And into the spirit get.
Listening to the talks and prayers,
You'll feel much better – I'll bet.

By Francis B. Mooneyhan Jr.
16 July 2008

FAITH

Faith is the substance hoped for,
The evidence of things not seen
The materials we know are out there
The things we hope to glean.

With faith all things are possible
To heal the sick or raise the dead
Accomplish many miracles
Such as you have never read.

With faith to walk on water
Just the way that Jesus did
But just like Peter, when it falters
He did sink when his faith slid.

It must be strong with nothing doubting
Holding strong to Christ, the Lord
Faith will lift us from our troubles
When we listen to His word.

HOPE

What do we have when we've lost everything?
When our dreams and ambitions are gone
When we've lost all that we love most
And all we can do is moan?

There's always something that will lift us up
And brings us from despair
It's hope, hope in something better
We know that Christ is there.

When we feel life's breath is gone
And we think with troubles we die
There is hope always there for us
And we find better days are nigh.

So be of good cheer, there's a way out
Of the problems we think there's no way
Hope is the answer, yet solved
It lifts to a brighter day.

By Francis B. Mooneyhan Jr.
July 18, 2008

THE HOUSE OF THE LORD

The temple is the house of the Lord
From there comes the latest word.
That's where He abides-And His spirit resides
For things we've never heard.

He's very particular in the leaders He chooses
To work in His Heavenly Home.
So they're chosen well-In the place where He dwells
So He isn't there alone.

For the work that is done there
Is through saints here on earth.
For the things that we learn-And the merits we earn
Are blessings of greater worth.

I have worked with these great men
Who served in our Columbia Temple.
I know or their worth-From the time of their birth
They have set a great example.

President Evans served well in performing his task
As his counselors were chosen with prayer.
He needed the best-When put to the test
For anyone serving there.

He chose Elder South and Elder Bass
To work with him side by side.
The testimonies of them-He knew wouldn't dim
In the house where God's spirit abides.

The matrons and sisters who also served
Contributed a lot to success
Their spirit and kindness-Was never a blindness
That kept them from doing their best.

As your mission ends-And another begins
We're thankful for the path you have trod.
For your work here on earth is of greatest worth
When you stay in the service of God.

By Francis B. Mooneyhan Jr.
September 8, 2008

MIRACLES

I believe in miracles
I see them every day.
To us they seem impossible
But that's Heavenly Father's way

The flowers in our garden
With fragrances so sweet
The bees that gather nectar
With sweetness that we eat

The raindrops fall so gently
To water grass and trees
The rainbow in the daytime
To promise and appease

The child that born to mother
A spirit from up above
Kind and tender treatment
To show a mother's love

The moon and stars that light the night
To show God's handiwork
They stretch out for beyond our dreams
Far beyond our search

The atom and electrons
That brings the world alive
The sunshine on the things we plant
To make them grow and thrive.

God comforts us when feeling blue
Heals us when we're sick
Does it through the priesthood
Without magic or a trick

Yes, I believe in miracles
They happen every day.
God made this world for you and me
He planned it all that way.

By Francis B. Mooneyhan Jr.
August 2008

MIRACLE OF THE GATE

When we received our mission call
To report the first of May
We were so excited
Looked forward to the day.

Arrived in Salt Lake City
And we were running late
I'd like to share the story of
The miracle of the gate.

Appointment time was running close
We searched for our abode.
Our car was packed up to the top
We need to unload

We had two cars to carry us
A friend came to assist
To leave our car parked on the street
Was hard then to resist.

We found the place we were to live
All safely locked up tight
To protect the occupants living there
Both day and then at night.

Enclosed all around it
With fences and a gate
To enter in you need a pass
Or just sit there and wait

We didn't know just what to do
We certainly couldn't wait
So with nothing else in mind
We pulled up to the gate

Lo and behold, it opened up to
Let both cars enter in
Relieved we were to get inside
And showed it with a grin.

We left one car and went our way
Exiting the gate
Hurried to our appointment
Before we were too late

Later on, when settling down
And talking to a friend,
We learned all tenants living there
Should have a pass to get them in.

I can't explain the events that day
When we were running late
All I can say, I'm thankful for
The miracle of the gate.

By Frances B. Mooneyhan
August 2008

IN THE TEMPLE

In the temple—serene and quiet
Hoping things will be all right
Interviewed with recommend
Waiting for the dividends

In God's house I like to be
Feeling the solemnity
Feeling that His spirit is there
Helps my thoughts to be aware

Aware of waiting spirits appealing
For some of us to do their sealing
Binding families to each other
Mother, dad, sister, brother

A vow, a promise to obey
Keep His laws till judgment day
The promise made in God's temple
To you may seem so very simple

But to God they all are real
They're meant to purify and heal
To draw us closer to His Son
To help us all to feel as one

In the temple are lots to learn
There exaltation you can earn
In the temple there is peace
Attendance helps your sins decrease.

By Francis B. Mooneyhan Jr.
October 17, 2008

TO THE UNCOMITTED

If you want to go to Heaven
Like you say you do
Then why not pay attention
To what God tells us to do.

He says unless you're baptized
You cannot enter in
Get the gift of the Holy Ghost
And then make Him your friend.

It really seems to me
You would want the greatest prize
To live with God and family
Some day in Paradise.

By Francis B Mooneyhan Jr.
2008

THE SABBATH

To rest from all our labors
A special day was given
To go to church and think of Christ
So our sins could be forgiven.

God gave us 7 days in all
Just one He wants for serving
Resting up to think of Him
So we'll be more deserving.

Be thankful for the Sabbath day
It was given you by God
To rest yourselves and rejuvenate
Not have to till the sod.

A day of worship to honor Him
By following through His plan
Accepting His son Jesus Christ
And serve our fellow man.

We're thankful for the Sabbath day
We serve with full intent
To help us find a better way
We take the sacrament.

To keep ourselves unspotted
On this our special day
To always have His spirit
In each and every way.

We sit in reverence and quietness
To listen to all that's said
By all the leaders over us
By song and things that's read.

We hope on this the Sabbath day
Through sacrament, word and hymn
We will take Christ in our hearts
And always remember Him.

By Francis B. Mooneyhan Jr.
October 12, 2008

Remembering Him

In Jesus name I now partake
The broken bread that has been brake
In memory of the only Son
That gave his life for everyone.

His broken body given free
Atoned for sins—both you and me
In memory of the blood, He gave.
To save us from the awful grave.

To lift and rescue each and all
Atone each one for Adam's fall
But we too must do our part
To help relieve His broken heart.

Our hearts and hands we must be sure
Will evermore be clean and pure.
Our actions help to ease the pain
If we're to live with Him again.

A broken heart for things we do
As these tokens we renew.
Remembering fully with real intent
The purpose of the sacrament.

He gave His all for you and me
So we with Him could ever be
As sons and daughters there restore
Live in glory ever more.

By Frances B. Mooneyhan Jr.
October 2008

219

GODS CHILDREN

God has sent us down to earth
To be His children at our birth

Loaned to parents to care and teach
Of His goodness they must preach.

Came from Heaven—now a child
With a goodness meek and mild

Not remembering from where we came
But from trials we get here we must tame.

Grow up stronger every day
Learn of Heavenly Father's way

Escape from Satan's temptation snare
Love our neighbor—learn to care.

Whatever the cause we have within
The power in self to cast out sin.

To live our lives—help from above
Share with others all our love.

At last to win the greater prize
And live with Him in paradise.

By Francis B. Mooneyhan Jr.
September 30, 2011

HE DID IT FOR US

Father in Heaven, in the name of Thy Son
Bless and sanctify us and help us be one.

Please bless the water and please bless the bread.
Help us be mindful of everything said.

As the sacred Sacrament we partake
Our thoughts of His body as it has been brake

In memory of His suffering as He shed His life's blood
Hoping we'll always remember His word.

That we may remember the sacrifice He gave
Redeem us and save us from the grips of the grave.

That His spirit will be with us to guide and direct
That we always love Him and give due respect.

He's our Savior, our God our Redeemer our all
He came to save us from Adam and Eve's fall.

So remember the Savior as the Sacrament you take
He did it for us, for your and my sake.

By Francis B. Mooneyhan Jr.
December 3, 2008

CONCERN FOR THE ONE

Salvation and Exaltation
And concern for the one
Is my missionary occupation
I won't stop until it's done.

Salvation is an individual matter
It's up to you alone
But when you break commandments
This the Lord will not condone.

God has given us our prophets,
Who we all must sustain.
We follow, love and honor them
And never him disdain.

God speaks to him and gives to him
Commandments we must keep.
Salvation comes from what we do.
We sow and we must reap.

Exaltation is a family matter.
We all must work together.
To teach and think of others
Not shackled by a tether.

To train a child in the way he should go
When old he will not depart.
Do it with love and gentle kindness
Always coming from the heart.

Home evenings, prayer and sharing love
By being an example
Seeking out our kindred dead
And going to the temple.

Church service helps in our endeavor
To care for and love each other.
All of us belong to God
Each sister and each brother.

Each one is special, each his own
With special need of kindness.
No thought of what they do or have
Or any earthly fineness.

Concern for one is what Christ did.
For one, He left the flock.
Each one is special in His sight
With love more solid than a rock.

Salvation free to all of us
Exaltation we must earn.
We accomplish this by what we do
And everything we learn.

Repent each day of things done wrong
Be kind in all you do.
Keep the commandments that you can
And God will bless and care for you.

By Francis B. Mooneyhan Jr.
July 24, 2008

222

SERVICE

Service to others
The key to our life
Help sisters and brothers
In relief of their strife.

Don't think of yourselves
And try to be greedy
Impart some to others
The poor and the needy.

Service to a widow
Alone with no spouse
All by themselves
Alone in their house.

The sick and the shut-ins
To suffer their ills
To sit all alone
While the cold winter chills

Relief Society and Priesthood
Were given by God
Another way of holding
To the pure Iron Rod

Don't wait for invitations
Do things on your own
And you'll build up rewards
For your Heavenly home

Service to others will cover
A multitude of sin
When you serve others
You feel good down with-in.

By Francis B. Mooneyhan Jr.
October 19, 2008

THE HOLY GHOST

Something we should desire
And covet the most
Is the power and influence
Of the Holy Ghost.

He's part of the Godhead
The Trinity
Not one of Himself
But part of The Three.

Each has their duty
Not repeating it twice
His purpose for us
Is to remind us of Christ.

Bring things to our remembrance
Of things we must know
To guide all our footsteps
Where ever we may go.

To be our companion
The whole daylong
And to be our conscious
When we start to do wrong.

He testifies of Jesus
Which brings us to God.
He helps us to hold on
To the Iron Rod.

A guide and a testator
A revealer of truth
To lead and refine us
From being uncouth.

So let's think more seriously
In our life, we need most
The constant companion
Of the Holy Ghost.

By Francis B. Mooneyhan Jr.

July 26 2008

JESUS LOVES ALL CHILDREN

JESUS loves all children
Black or white or brown
He loves to hear their prayers
And never turns them down

Although they're spread across the world
Their hearts are all sincere
Different languages they speak
Each one of them He hears.

No respecter of just one
He treats them all the same.
He loves each and everyone
And knows them all by name.

By Francis B. Mooneyhan Jr.
January 14, 2009

GIVING THANKS

Jesus is more sensitive than we
He made Heaven and the Earth.
He's concerned in what we think and do
And has been since our birth

He likes to know we're happy
And what He's done for us is right
There are many things we're asking for
We're pleading day and night.

We're always asking—never thanking
That causes Him concern.
Like the time He healed 10 lepers
9 of them 'thanks' did not return.

We need to find a thankful time
Sometime within our week
To not ask but give our 'thanks'
For all those things we seek.

If we just think how blessed we are
More so than many others
Family, friends, good health and such
Not burdened down with troubles

To see, to hear, to walk and run
To live in the USA
Just to have good water to drink
To watch our children run and play

Oh how greatly blessed we are
No fear of war or tanks
We need to set one day aside
And give our Lord our thanks.

By Francis B. Mooneyhan Jr.
February 26, 2009

227

A SPECIAL GIFT

A guiding star came from afar
To show the place of birth
A guiding light to set aright
The Savior here on Earth.

To our heart—a humble start
To usher in great peace
Because of Him—no more would dim
Our hopes but just increase

Gifts He brings to poor and kings
Is equal for us all
What we need—to do is heed
His voice when he does call.

The shinning ray that shines today
For all the world to see
Came at His birth—to all on Earth
His gift to you and me.

By Francis B. Mooneyhan Jr.
December 11, 2008

A WORLD FOR US

Assignment from the Father
Given to His Son
Make an earth for His children
Convenient for everyone

Water water everywhere
Give lots for all to drink
But let them labor for a while.
He wants to make us think.

Put some ore within the ground
For us to melt and mold.
For a monetary system
Use silver and some gold.

To get around up in the sky,
We need magnetic lines
To give direction and protect the earth
From pole to pole will do just fine.

Magnetic fields for electricity
To brighten up the night
Trees and flowers everywhere
To enhance our sight

He gave us atoms and electrons
To give us light and sound
Making cars, trains and planes
For us to get around

What a grand world He did make
He did it not abrupt
Just be glad and use it wisely
Don't try to mess it up.

By Francis B. Mooneyhan Jr.
April 22-2009

TABERNACLE CHOIR

There's a program aired each Sunday
Called, "Music and the Spoken Word"
The message and the music
Such as you have never heard.

Awe, inspiring and uplifting
Gets you started for the week
Helps you more to think of others
Uplifts the spirit that you seek.

As you think of time and practice
By each member of the choir
Just to bring you satisfaction
Sundays for one half an hour.

Some continue working
And some of them retire
But all are thrilled to sing
In the Tabernacle Choir.

They all have one thing in common
A great desire to sing
To raise their voices to the Lord
The joy and peace that music brings.

By Francis B. Mooneyhan Jr.
2009

TEMPLE SQUARE

If you come to Salt Lake City
For a while remaining there
You should give some serious thoughts
To visit temple square.

There's much history gathered there
To whet your appetite
There's much effort to make sure
All that's said is right.

The information that you find
Will be the very best
You'll find the reason why the saints
Migrated to the west.

The peace and harmony there abound
With beauty everywhere
Flowers and fountains all around
For your pleasure there.

Information you will find
Free tours are set for you
All these things to ease your mind
In everything you do.

If you decide to learn of Christ
Or doctrines we believe
These, too, are available
With booklets you receive.

So when you visit Salt Lake City
New treasures you will find
As you tour on Temple Square
You'll ease and brighten up your mind.

By Francis B. Mooneyhan Jr.
2009

EFFECTS OF JOSEPH'S PRAYER

A meek young boy of fourteen
Went in the woods to pray.
The marvelous things he learned
Are with us to this day.

He learned for sure there is a God
In Heaven up above
That He's aware of us on earth
And showers us with love.

He saw the Father and the Son.
They looked like you and I.
With a body of flesh and bones
But more glorious from on high.

He conversed with Jesus Christ
We know that they will speak
To special ones here on earth
When our need for them we seek.

He gave instructions for a church
To us in latter days
To lead, guide and teach us
Of His laws and ways.

A lot of glorious truths were learned
On that eventful day
When a lad of just 14
Went in the woods to pray.

By Francis B. Mooneyhan
May 1-2009

SEASONS

Christmas Greeting 1969
Christmas Greetings from Mooneyhans 1976
The Greatest Gift 2004
It's Christmas Time (2006)
It's That Time Of Year Again 2006
It's Christmas Time Again 2006
Waiting On Santa 2006
Fall Best Time of the year 2008
Halloween 2008

First Snow Fall2008
Winter 2008
Christmas Lights On Temple Square
Christmas Devotional (12-8-08)
Christmas Greeting 2008
Christmas Time Is Here 2008
White Christmas 2008
Christmas Lights (12-24-08)
Christmas Away From home 2008
Mission Friends Christmas Greeting 2008
A New Year 2009
Conservation Lab Valentine
Springtime 2009
Easter 2009
Summer 2009
Fall is Here (10-5-11)

CHRISTMAS GREETING 1969

In making sure you get a card
And helping postmen too
We'll write a note to show we care
And hand this card to you.

We're taking very special care
This year to tell our friends
How much their friendship means to us
Right now as this year ends.

So may the lord be good to you
And bless in every way
To see you safe and well right now
And on through Christmas day

With every blessing that you need
For all the family too
We're sending all the love we have
From the Mooneyhans to you.

By Francis B. Mooneyhan
1969

CHRISTMAS GREETING 1976

It's that time of year again
I feel so melancholy
Seeing all the Christmas things
With mistletoe and holly.

People running everywhere
Not taking time for stopping
They only have one thing in mind
To finish up their shopping.

My shopping's very simple-so
I'll get it off my chest
I'm wishing all my friends this year
The happiest and the best.

I hope this season brings to you
The best in every way
Good health, and love and peace of mind
And joy on Christmas day.

May God abide within your home
And all throughout the lands
Merry Christmas to all of you
From all the Mooneyhans

By Frances B. Mooneyhan
Circa 1976

THE GREATEST GIFT

It's that time of year again
And all of us are busy
At 869 Pebble Lane
With Kitty, Frank and Lizzie

Stringing lights on Christmas tree
With Mistletoe and Holley
Shopping late and buying gifts
Makes us feel so jolly

The greatest gift to all the world
Came on Christmas day
When Jesus Christ, our Lord, was born
In a manger on the hay

Of all the gifts we think we need
The greatest gift is love
Like the gift God sent to us
By His Son from up above

So Merry Christmas everyone
And a Happy New Year too
May God's richest blessing be
With family and friends like you

By Francis B. Mooneyhan Jr.
December 2004

THAT TIME OF YEAR AGAIN

It's that time of year again
When all of us are busy
Thinking of all the things to do
Really makes me dizzy

Remembering friends like you is easy
You come to mind real fast
You and me good fiends forever
Good friends are made to last.

So Merry Christmas to all of you
And all throughout the land
A happy New Year greeting
From all the Mooneyhans

By Francis B. Mooneyhan Jr.

2006

IT'S CHRISTMAS TIME AGAIN

It's Christmas time again
The month that I love best
Just thinking of all the things to do
Can't really find much rest

Trying to find a gift for all
Not just anything will do.
The most important gift I give
Will be the one for you

My warmest wish and deepest love
I hold for you alone
May this warmth and love abide
With family, friends and home

May God look down and smile
Upon all your family too
May next year be the best year yet
For family and friends like you

By Francis B. Mooneyhan Jr.
December 2006

WAITING ON SANTA

T'was the night before Christmas
And all over town
Most other folks
Were just fooling around

But not the Mooneyhan family
For they knew on this night
That any minute now
Santa could come into site.

So we all were very quiet
As we were milling around
Anxiously waiting for Santa
To come into town.

Someone saw him in Lugoff
Which I have nothing against
Headed for the Camden church
Of the Latter Day Saints.

Where families are together
And all having fun
Mother and daughter
Father and son.

Families are forever
And this Santa knows
He loves good boys and girls
That's where he always goes.

So be real still and listen
And I think you all will hear
The sound of Santa coming
To visit all of you this year.

By Francis B. Mooneyhan Jr.
December 2006

FALL—THE BEST TIME OF THE YEAR

Summer's gone and fall is here
You can tell by the trees.
Every year about this time
They start giving up their leaves.

The days are warm—the nights are cold
The moon above, great depth
The colors on the mountains
Will nearly take your breath

Not too hot—not too cold
The best months of them all
Of all the seasons of the year
I really like the fall.

Camping trips and football games
A great time of the year
Perfect for families
Which makes the season dear

The Harvest Moon from up above
Gives off a golden sheen
Not long from now—a few weeks more
We celebrate Halloween.

The month after the end of fall
Thanksgiving time is near
We celebrate without gift giving
The best time of the year

By Frank Mooneyhan Jr.
Fall 2008

HALLOWEEN 2008

How do you like Halloween?
When ghosts and goblins rant and scream
Children run from door to door
Filling bags and wanting more

"Trick or treat", you hear them scream
Each and every Halloween
Running up and down the streets
Trying to fill their bags with treats

Wearing costumes—every kind
Some would even blow your mind
All of this comes every fall
Some have fun but not for all

Scary stuff's not for old age
It sometimes puts me in a rage
Years ago before my teens
Even I liked Halloween

By Francis B. Mooneyhan Jr.
October 17, 2008

THE FIRST SNOW FALL

Overnight-what a beautiful sight
For us to wake up to
On the ground and all around
Was a site for me and you.

Early fall gave up it's all
And finally gave in to winter
For overnight a blanket of white
Upon our lawn did enter.

The pure white snow did have a glow
And white was everywhere
It seemed to clean and have sheen
And cover <u>all</u> out there.

Oh happy sight, this overnight
Surprise was quite so dear
It was to me so good to see
The first snowfall this year

By Francis B. Mooneyhan Jr.
October 12, 2008

WINTER

Winter is here
With it, good news and bad
Some of us happy
Some of us sad.

Some think of its misery
With cold everywhere
The bone chilling cold
With not enough clothes to wear.

Some think of winter
As being lots of fun
Great family activities
For most every one.

Ice skating and skiing
Building snowmen too
Hiking and sledding
There's plenty to do.

There's a purpose for winter
And God has His reason
As all things in nature
Each has its season.

The flowers and trees
Need a break from the summer
It's time for a rest
It's time for a slumber.

Rejuvenate themselves
The joys they bring
And try to be ready
For the coming of spring.

So try to be thankful
As each season enters
There's a purpose from God
As He gives us good winters.

Winter has come
And winter is fun
There's plenty to do
For most everyone

Sledding and skiing
Building snowmen too
Activities together
There's plenty to do.

Cuddle up closer
By a nice roaring fire
Drinking hot chocolate
And sing till we tire.

Sit in the park
And watch the snowfall
Amazed at the whiteness
As it covers all.

Dressed warn in a toboggan
Snowball fights on the lawn
You feel as this season
Is your very own.

Going caroling at Christmas
Serenading our friends
Cuddled closely on sleigh rides
The fun never ends.

Take a deep breath
Let the crisp air enter
We sure are thankful
For this fun-filled winter.

By Francis B. Mooneyhan Jr.
October 15, 2008

CHRISTMAS LIGHTS ON TEMPLE SQUARE

It makes us all so happy
To see it lit up so
Emphasizing our surroundings
With everything aglow.

It's like each light's an angel
Way up in the trees
They then appear as dancing
Whenever there's a breeze.

They bring to mind a season
That happens every year
Long ago a child was born
A star was shown so clear.

Christ the Lord was born on earth
A star showed all the way.
And now with lights we celebrate
The Son on Christmas day.

As the lights an ensign
To celebrate the gift
To lighten hearts of each of us
And give us all a lift.

So let your mind and thoughts run wild
As you walk around out there.
Enjoy the season and the awe
Of lights on Temple Square.

By Francis B. Mooneyhan
November 2008

CHRISTMAS DEVVOTIONAL

Christmas devotional is given each year.
By the general authorities of things we need to hear.

The joys of Christmas and songs of the season
The message of Christ to give us good reason

The songs and the lights for our celebration
Helps us to be glad to have this occasion.

To celebrate His birth and remember the reason
We need to be happy this holiday season

Now is the time for our gift giving
To those in need, gives a reason for living.

Bells, songs and lights penetrate the air
As millions of saints celebrate everywhere.

It's a time for Christmas, a time to be gay
A time to be joyous on this Christmas day.

A time to be happy, a time to be nice
A time to celebrate the birth of our Christ.

By Francis B. Mooneyhan Jr.
December 8, 2008

Christmas Greetings

Christmas Blessings

Season's greetings to you all
It's that time of year
Be thankful for the year that's past
And think ahead with cheer.

A time of year for giving thanks
And having family fun
Thinking of the ones we love
Remembering everyone.

Reaching deep within our hearts
And hope we're not too greedy
With all the gifts we get and give
Impart some to the needy.

The time of year when Christ was born
To save us all from sin
We hope His spirit will touch us all
And let Him enter in.

Without the Christ in Christmas
Leaves the season bare
There's no hope to celebrate
Here or anywhere.

So count your blessings one by one
Be thankful for His birth.
He brings us peace and joy today
For us and all the earth.

Christmas Friendships

It's that time of year again
With mistletoe and holly
Time for gaiety and fun
A time for being jolly.

A time to think of everyone
Our friends and loved ones too
This time of year is special
That's why we think of you.

The Lord has been so good this year
It seems it never ends
He gives us health and strength to serve
And lots of real good friends.

It's good to reach this time of year
We think it's really great
The blessings that has come to us
And Christ's birth to celebrate.

I'm thankful for your friendship
It means a lot to me
I hope that it will be this way
For all eternity.

We send our love and best to you
With joy as best we can
Merry Christmas to you all
From Frank and Kitty Mooneyhan.

By Frances B. Mooneyhan Jr.

CHRISTMAS TIME IS HERE

We run around in shopping malls
Buying gifts for everyone
Hoping no one is forgotten
Still having lots of fun

This time of year is wonderful
With mistletoe and holly
Remembering friends and loving family
And really being jolly

I believe I've thought of everyone
Not sure of all their needs
More time well spent on other things
Like doing more good deeds

Thinking of others—that's the key
The things that bring good cheer
Just like Christ to lift up others
The gift that lasts all year

Life on earth is a gift from God
We need to make it great
Being with family and special friends
All other things can wait.

Quality time and quality deeds
Just do—not thinking twice
Think of others—not yourself
And try to be like Christ.

That way the Christmas Spirit
Will seem more true and dear
And you will feel much better now
And all throughout the year.

By Francis B. Mooneyhan Jr.
December 14, 2008

WHITE CHRISTMAS

We had a White Christmas this year
The first I ever recall.
Back in the south where the weather is warmer
We seldom see snow at all.

It's nice to see the white stuff around
With kids scurrying about.
Most people really enjoy the event
Some older folks could just do without.

It sure does make a difference to most
As it whitens and cleans all around
Covers the dirty, makes everything shiny
And beautifies all the town.

Snowball fights and horse drawn sleighs
Snowmen of every kind
Walking hand in hand together
Humming songs within your mind.

Skiing the slopes and sledding downhill
Walking hand in hand in the park
Enjoying the beauty that nature has brought
And lingering outside after dark.

The lights at night has a different glow
As they shine and flicker on ice
Everything's covered in a white fluffy coat
Makes you feel cozy and nice.

You take opportunities to enjoy all things
That God has put down below
White Christmas is one of the holidays I've had
I've really enjoyed it so.

By Francis B. Mooneyhan Jr.
December 18-2008

CHRISTMAS LIGHTS

Christmas lights
Are used each year
To decorate
And bring forth cheer.

They're scattered out
In many places
Brings gleeful smiles
On children's faces

Strung along on
Christmas trees
To bring more color
And also to please

Placed on city
Streets at night
Oh what a glorious
Pleasant sight

Strung in trees
On temple square
For all to enjoy
Who visit there

Around the world
Those lit up nights
I'm thankful for
The Christmas lights

By Francis B. Mooneyhan Jr.
December 24, 2008

CHRISTMAS AWAY FROM HOME

This time of year when Christmas comes
There are changes everywhere.
People have a change of heart
There's music in the air.

We tend to think lots more of sharing
With family, friends and others
Our hearts are soften towards the poor
They, too, indeed our brothers

But mostly we just settle down
With family and our friends
Hope we keep them ever close
And friendship never ends.

Christmas is not the same this year.
We are far away
Far away from those we love
To celebrate Christmas day.

But you are always in our hearts
No matter where we roam.
We can do real fine right now
Can celebrate when we get home.

By Francis B. Mooneyhan Jr.
December 11, 2008

MISSION FRIENDS CHRISTMAS GREETING 2008

This year we've taken special care
While we're on our mission
To see that you and all of yours
Will give us your permission

To give each one our love to you
And let you know we care
Because you are such special friends
We've met most anywhere.

A thought has entered in
To the message for this year
We want to show our love for you
And send to you good cheer.

Christmas is a special time
And you are special too
That's why we want to tell
How much we think of you

Of all the choicest friends we have
We hold you each so dear.
Glad we are to associate
And work with you so near.

Just like to send our Christmas wish
And love as best we can.
We hope this year brings joy to you
From Frank and Kitty Mooneyhan

By Francis B. Mooneyhan Jr.
December 10, 2008

NEW YEAR 2009

The New Year is here
And Christmas is gone
We seem to forget
What this has brought on

We've forgotten CHRIST's birthday
And looking ahead
To a new year of troubles
With things that we dread

Gasoline prices
And wars in the East
Talk of depression
Sure makes things look bleak

Most of the time
Our own troubles we make
And blame it on others
Past solutions don't take.

If we would read our scriptures
From the prophets take advice
We never would have to
Make the same mistake twice

But another year comes
And we make resolutions
To make this year better
With our very own solutions

So, Happy New Year
I hope you can do it.
There's lots to be done
So you had better hop to it!

By Francis B. Mooneyhan Jr.
December 31, 2008

253

CONSERVATION LAB VALENTINE

That special day is here again
It comes just once a year.
We pay homage to those we love
And those we hold so dear.

Attention all you females
Whom we hold so kind.
Asking each and every one
To be our Valentine.

Don't know the one who started this.
The idea was not bad
It gives us males a chance each year
To be Sir Galahad.

Each of us have special ones
We like to claim as "Mine".
You know who you are out there
Won't you be our Valentine?

By Francis B. Mooneyhan Jr.
February 12, 2009

SPRING

SPRING TIME

All winter trees and flowers sleep
Protected from the cold
The warmth of spring arouse them
Their beauties to un-fold.

Spring is great for many reasons
It brings the world alive.
Nature slept, but now awakes
From winter woes survived.

Grass and flowers everywhere
Budding trees abound.
Birds are singing from the trees
You feel the gladness all around.

A new growth process has begun
To replenish and renew
For food and beauty, peace of mind
All of this for me and you.

The warmth of sun upon your face
A chance to get outside
More activities out with nature
A lot less time confined inside.

So get outside in sun or rain
Enjoy the air so clean.
Just be thankful once again.
The Lord has given spring.

SPRING 2009

Spring 09 has come around
To thaw up all the frozen ground.

Flowers, trees, all things that grow
Sleep all winter beneath the snow.

All winter long their strength was kept
Now wakens all of them that slept.

Warmth of sunshine makes them rise
To change in beauty, shape and size.

To make this happen once again
Requires a drink of gentle rain.

The winds that blow a gentle shake
Reminds each one, time to awake.

Partake of sun and rain to grow
Rise above the fallen snow.

Time to beautify the earth
Expand with all your greatest worth.

Join the birds wherever they sing
Reminds us all it's time for spring.

By Francis B. Mooneyhan
March 26, 2009

EASTER

On a glorious Easter morn
For this day was Jesus born.

For the sacrifice for sin
Atonement so we all could win

To give His life and suffer pain
So each of us can live again.

Thanks be to Him that He has risen
Has broken from His 3 day prison.

Scoffed and scorned, no heed His plea
His atonement was for you and me.

Thankful all that we should be.
Christ's sacrifice for you and me.

All that's required of us by Him
Never let His light grow dim.

For you and me, we each were born
To share with Christ the Easter morn

To share with Him the sacrifice,
Never to endure it twice.

Accept the atonement for us all
Good or bad – large or small.

God the Father's only son
Sacrificed for everyone.

He paid the price for Adam's sin
For you and me, so let Him in.

His sacrifice for you and me
To be with Him eternally.

By Francis B. Mooneyhan Jr.
March 11, 2009

SUMMER

Summer is here
And it's hot as a stew
But that's not saying
There's nothing to do

Great times for all
When the day's work is done
Go out by the pool
And lay in the sun.

Swimming and boating,
Hiking and fishing,
Tending your garden
Or just sitting and wishing

It's a time for renewing
As the bees start their swarming
Spreading pollen in flowers
As the days start warming.

As you warm in the sunshine
You know there's a cost
It won't be too long
Before there's a big frost.

So be glad for the summer
And look forward to fall
Try to determine
Which is better for all.

By Francis B. Mooneyhan Jr.
July 17-2009

FALL IS HERE-2011

Summer's gone and fall is here
There's cooler days and nights.
The foliage of the hills and dales
Are showing off their sights.

Abundant flowers once in bloom
Are fewer now in number.
For all the beauty they once had
It's time for them to slumber.

Fall is time for slowing down
The seeds in earth must enter.
All of nature must be prepared
To rest throughout the winter.

By Francis B. Mooneyhan Jr.
October 5, 2011

CPSIA information can be obtained at www.ICGtesting.com
Printed in the USA
LVOW080210140412

277568LV00001B/12/P